AMERICA'S PASTIME ON THE BRINK OF WAR

MARTIN W. SANDLER and **CRAIG SANDLER**

BLOOMSBURY
CHILDREN'S BOOKS
NEW YORK LONDON OXFORD NEW DELHI SYDNEY

For Jill, Laura, Lila, Scott and Susan—
and for each other.

BLOOMSBURY CHILDREN'S BOOKS
Bloomsbury Publishing Inc., part of Bloomsbury Publishing Plc
1359 Broadway, New York, NY 10018
50 Bedford Square, London, WC1B 3DP, UK
Bloomsbury Publishing Ireland Limited, 29 Earlsfort Terrace, Dublin 2, D02 AY28, Ireland

BLOOMSBURY, BLOOMSBURY CHILDREN'S BOOKS, and the Diana logo
are trademarks of Bloomsbury Publishing Plc

First published in the United States of America in April 2026
by Bloomsbury Children's Books

Text copyright © 2026 by Martin W. Sandler and Craig Sandler

All rights reserved. No part of this publication may be: i) reproduced or transmitted in any form, electronic or mechanical, including photocopying, recording, or by means of any information storage or retrieval system without prior permission in writing from the publishers; or ii) used or reproduced in any way for the training, development, or operation of artificial intelligence (AI) technologies, including generative AI technologies. The rights holders expressly reserve this publication from the text and data mining exception as per Article 4(3) of the Digital Single Market Directive (EU) 2019/790.

Bloomsbury books may be purchased for business or promotional use. For information on bulk purchases please contact Macmillan Corporate and Premium Sales Department at specialmarkets@macmillan.com

Library of Congress Cataloging-in-Publication Data
available upon request
ISBN 978-1-5476-0797-6 (hardcover) • ISBN 978-1-5476-1418-9 (e-book)

Book design by Patrick and Diane M. Collins
Printed and bound in China
2 4 6 8 10 9 7 5 3 1

To find out more about our authors and books visit www.bloomsbury.com and sign up for our newsletters.
For product safety–related questions contact productsafety@bloomsbury.com.

CONTENTS

Introduction	iv
1 ✦ BASEBALL ON THE BRINK	1
2 ✦ THE STREAK	21
3 ✦ THE KID	43
4 ✦ SEPIA BALL	63
5 ✦ THE WORLD SERIES	95
6 ✦ BASEBALL GOES TO WAR	115
7 ✦ JAPAN AND BASEBALL	139
8 ✦ THE FUTURE BEGINS	157
Further Reading for Each Chapter	175
Sources	177
Acknowledgments	179
Photograph Credits	179
Index	180

INTRODUCTION

AMERICANS HAVE ALWAYS seemed to need baseball, and in the spring of 1941, America needed baseball more than ever. Most of the world was consumed by war that spring, and the great nations of Europe and Asia were falling to fascists. Japan—the only nation that loved baseball as much as America did, perhaps more—would engulf the United States in the Second World War just weeks after the 1941 World Series. Both the game and the nation were about to change forever.

But in springtime 1941, that was still to come. Spring in America had always meant the chance to go out and play a game of baseball, or a few innings, or at least a game of catch. On the small-town diamonds, the big-city sandlots, the college stadiums, the minor league fields, kids of every size and shape and description turned out to play. And many more of them were watching.

Baseball was truly "the national pastime." Each new season brought nearly ten million people out to major-league ballparks, while hundreds of millions more followed their beloved teams through radio, newspapers, and magazines. For these fans, the arrival of spring meant the resumption of life's greatest joy.

Not an empty seat to be found! Spectators pack Yankee Stadium during the remarkable World Series that capped off one of the most extraordinary seasons in major league history.

INTRODUCTION ◆ v

And with the coming of this particular spring, Americans were very short on joy. The first peacetime draft in American history was already pulling hundreds of thousands of young men away from their hometowns and families, and there seemed little doubt they would soon be facing fire overseas.

THE NATION STOPPED WHAT IT WAS DOING AND HELD ITS BREATH AS JOE DIMAGGIO AND TED WILLIAMS ACCOMPLISHED THE UNMATCHABLE.

There, the war had been raging for years. Nazi Germany and Fascist Italy already ruled much of Europe, and had England and America in their sights. Japan held much of Asia, China included. Everyone knew Japan was thinking about striking at America next; no one seriously imagined it would happen that very fall, but by spring 1941, the sense of daily dread that filled most American hearts was justified.

THE VERY FIRST MAJOR LEAGUER drafted for the war effort was Hugh "Losing Pitcher" Mulcahy of the Philadelphia Phillies, called to service on March 8, 1941. He'd earned the nickname by losing twenty games in 1938 and twenty-two games in 1940. He never posted a winning season. But Mulcahy won the nation's heart with his dutiful response to being called up. "My losing streak is over," he told reporters. "I'm on a winning team now."

A few weeks later, on April 21, 1941, the Yankees beat the Philadelphia Athletics, 14-4. In the same week, the nation of Greece surrendered to Fascist Italy and Nazi Germany. As it would turn out, that would not be unusual for the 1941 season: as profound calamities unfolded worldwide, Americans turned to their beloved pastime as a respite.

And amazingly, with darkness closing in all over the world, baseball staged a season that still shines in the annals of this history-obsessed sport as one of the brightest seasons ever, maybe the brightest. This book is the story of that season.

The story of 1941 is the story of two young men on opposite sides of the game's fiercest rivalry who crossed from greatness into immortality by setting records that have never been equaled in the more than eighty years since. The nation stopped what it was doing and held its breath as Joe DiMaggio and Ted Williams accomplished the unmatchable.

The story of 1941 is the story of a World Series headlined by two teams from New York: a club that seemed to appear in the Fall Classic every year and a team that—despite having the most loyal, nuttiest, and raucous fans in the league—hadn't come anywhere close to the World Series for twenty years. And the contest would be defined not by some clutch home run or dazzling fielding play but by the most colossal blunder in World Series history.

The story of 1941 is also the story of baseball in a segregated, fiercely racist America—where the major leagues did not permit Black players and, in many cases, Black fans in the stadiums. So it's the story of separate leagues—the all-white major leagues and a Black baseball system that featured players who would have been among the best on any major league roster had they been allowed to play there.

And the story of 1941 includes the moment that women got "a league of their own," a league that would captivate fans through the war years and beyond. These indomitable athletes made their mark on baseball history and paved the way for greater opportunities for women in athletics and society for decades to come.

The heroes at home and the horrors abroad, the knowledge that life was about to change forever, and the way the players responded—all made summer 1941 a singularly shining season. Baseball had been there for Americans for two hundred years, in one form or another, in good times and bad. This was one of the worst. And it was at this moment that baseball reached for, and delivered, its best.

BASEBALL ON THE BRINK

AS THE PROFESSIONAL BASEBALL world gathered for the 1941 season, the game and the nation were still recovering from their last significant crisis. The Great Depression of the 1930s, which had left a quarter of American workers unemployed, had also been difficult for baseball and its teams. Attendance at games had plunged by as much as 40 percent. Many clubs in the minor leagues and the Negro Leagues had folded. By 1940, the economy had recovered enough that attendance almost hit the ten million mark, which it hadn't done in several years. So, while everyone in baseball, and in America, was troubled by a terrible war creeping ever so closer to the United States, there was some joy and relief as well.

Every year, then as now, warming temperatures meant a new baseball season was just around the corner. In April 1941, the major league teams gathered down south for spring training, just as teams had done since the 1870s. There were few signs of dread there—just calisthenics and fielding practice and running drills and horsing around. True, a

Major league baseball games have long provided opportunities to display collective national pride.

handful of players were pulled out of camp for the military draft, but for the most part things felt normal.

"Normal" in America in 1941 was vastly different from today. This was a world without jet planes or plastic toys or McDonald's or interstate highways. Computers were fifty years away from entering the home. There were no cell phones, there were no video games, and television was an exotic new invention. At the corner store, a bottle of Coke cost five cents. So did a hot dog at a ball game. Life *felt* different too. It was quieter, slower. People had more faith in their government, in the news media, and in institutions of all kinds.

At a time when major league salaries were much lower than today, Ernie Banks, star shortstop for the Chicago Cubs, had an offseason job as a car salesman.

That included baseball: People believed what they read about the heroes of the diamond, and very little of what was written was negative. Media coverage was less intense and more cheerful. There were no millionaire ballplayers either—with no enormous television revenue to bolster ball clubs' payrolls and no free agency allowing ballplayers to sell their services to the highest bidder, players' salaries were modest. In fact, the typical big leaguer earned so little that he needed to work all winter, as a bartender or store clerk or repairman—in a regular job.

Imagine walking into a hardware store during the off season today and having Aaron Judge sell you a hammer or a garden hose, or wandering into a clothing store and buying a tie from Mookie Betts. It seems unbelievable.

Nowadays, when spring training ends and teams travel north for opening day, players who earn millions of dollars a season board special team airplanes and fly to opening day in luxury. But as the 1941 season began, the players gathered at the train stations in Florida, Texas, and California for journeys that might take days—in railroad cars where big leaguers mingled with starstruck fellow passengers. "I recall playing a doubleheader in Pittsburgh on a Sunday in late August in 1941, while we were in a pennant race with the Dodgers, then riding the train all night to play a morning exhibition game in Stamford, Connecticut, against a semi-pro team," recalled former Cardinal star outfielder Terry Moore. "After the morning game, we got back on the train and rode on to Boston, where our cars were uncoupled and we were shunted to a siding so we could get some more sleep before playing another game that same afternoon."

> ...SOME OF THE GREATEST MAJOR LEAGUE PARKS, LIKE YANKEE STADIUM, HAD NO LIGHTS AT ALL.

There was no question that it was difficult. But for some players, there was a real upside to all this travel by train. Infielder Don Gutteridge was one of them. "It took a lot longer than it does now," he remembered, "but I loved traveling across the country by train. It resulted in a far greater camaraderie than you have on ball clubs today because you spent so much time together. We ate together in the dining car, played cards together, slept together in the [sleeping cars] and talked baseball by the hour."

Logistical differences abounded: Almost every game was played in the afternoon, and some of the greatest major league parks, like Yankee Stadium, had no lights at all. There were only eight teams in each league, half as many as today. Not a single club was located farther west than St. Louis. There were no playoffs in October. "Wild card" was a poker term, having nothing to do with team sports or choosing champions. After the regular season ended, the

The radio was a fixture in most American homes by 1941. Many women became baseball fans by listening to day games on the radio.

World Series started immediately. The first-place finisher in the American League played the first-place finisher in the National League—and that was it.

In 1941 being a fan was also notably different than today. With no television, the only way of seeing your major league team in action was to be at the ballpark. But in 1941, with almost ten percent of the nation still out of work as the Depression lingered, a ticket to a major league game remained an unaffordable luxury for many. There was, however, radio—a part of family life in most American homes by 1941. People would gather around the radio sets the way they do today around the TV and listen to crime and mystery dramas, comedy, and variety shows.

4 ♦ BASEBALL'S SHINING SEASON

Baseball broadcasting was new, and not without controversy. Some teams, like the Yankees, felt that giving the games away "for free" by broadcasting them live on the radio would keep fans from buying tickets and attending the games in person. So they broadcast no games at all. Other ball clubs, however, most notably the Dodgers and the Reds, discovered that broadcasting the games built interest in the teams and actually boosted attendance. And there was one now-forgotten consequence of nearly all broadcasts coming in the daytime, with most dads out of the house and at work and kids at school or at play: an ever-growing segment of the baseball audience was women.

As for the kids, theirs was also a much different world than it is today. "I heard on the radio," Joe Diaz of the *Des Moines Register* wrote in 2015, "that a reporter from the *Philadelphia Inquirer* traveled the entire country for quite some time looking for a game of pickup baseball. Sadly he didn't find one. Not even one!" In summertime 1941, by contrast, kids were likely to play baseball on every vacant lot in every city and town in America. Every day, all summer long, it seemed, there was a pickup game of baseball going on. After a quick trip home for lunch, the game would resume and continue until it was too dark to see the ball. And throughout all this ball play, there was not a single adult to be seen.

Like millions of other kids throughout America, a youngster takes part in a sandlot baseball game.

Actually, kids' pickup games were not the only kind of so-called sandlot games being played. From the beginning of the 1900s until the years following World War II, adult teams representing towns, workplaces, churches, and social clubs played in local leagues throughout the nation. These semiprofessional teams played most of the baseball that Americans got to see with their own eyes, since very few had the means to travel to the major metropolitan areas where the big leaguers played. Frequently thousands, and sometimes tens of thousands, turned out to watch their local teams play.

Of all the differences between baseball in 1941 and

baseball today, the most visible difference of all was also the most damning. In 1941, in a nation where some of the greatest ballplayers were Black, Black athletes played in a separate league because white members of their own nation were too racist to include them.

Actually, in 1941, segregation and the racial prejudice that spawned it was only one of the major problems that Americans faced. In a world growing smaller with each passing year, the war in Europe was getting more devastating with each passing day. "Devastating" was, in fact, too mild of a word. Under the leadership of Chancellor Adolf Hitler, a man intent on world domination, German military forces had been invading and conquering one country after another. Lights had gone out throughout the continent. Millions of people had been killed or imprisoned. Nation after nation had lost its freedom.

It had all happened with terrifying speed. In March 1939, Germany had taken over Czechoslovakia. Later that same year, after only a month of fighting, German troops had destroyed Poland. By May 1940, Denmark, Norway, Belgium, Luxembourg, and the Netherlands had all fallen to Hitler's troops. Then in June 1940, the biggest blow thus far—the fall of France.

With almost all of Continental Europe under his control, Hitler turned his attention to America's greatest and dearest ally, England. On September 7, 1940, the German air force, known as the Luftwaffe, began conducting

In 1914, 100,000 fans attended the amateur championship game between Telling's Strollers and Hanna's Cleaners at Brookside Stadium in Cleveland, Ohio.

horrific bombing raids on London and other vital British cities such as Liverpool and Birmingham, all with the intent of forcing a British surrender. Six days after the bombing of these cities began, a whole new theater of war was opened in Africa when Germany's ally Italy invaded Egypt.

On December 29, 1940, President Franklin D. Roosevelt took to the radio to give another of what had come to be called "fireside chats." It was the most direct talk he had yet given about the European conflict. No one was more aware of the grave situation in Europe than Roosevelt. Yet, he also knew that most Americans fervently wanted the country to stay out of the war.

Although he made it clear that he would do everything humanly possible to avoid military engagement, the president emphatically declared that the United States would become an "arsenal of democracy," selling military supplies to England that it desperately needed to fight Germany. It was a bold declaration, backed by an equally bold policy that brought the United States as close to the war as possible without engaging in the actual fighting.

Meanwhile, things in the Pacific had become extremely ominous as well. For decades, militant Japanese leaders had endeavored to expand their empire and turn their island nation into a world power. In 1931, Japan had forcibly taken over Manchuria. In 1937, it had invaded part of China, capturing the capital city of Nanjing and advancing deeper into that huge country. Beginning in late September 1940, after Japan signed an alliance with Germany and

BASEBALL ON THE BRINK ◆ 7

A DIFFERENT GAME

It was still pitcher against batter. The mound was still sixty feet, six inches from home plate. The bases were still ninety feet apart. But there were many things that made baseball in 1941 different from what it is today.

- **IN 1941,** as had been the case since the major leagues began, every ruling on the field was made by an umpire, with no opportunity to appeal his judgment. Instant replay, so much a part of the game today, hadn't been imagined.

- **IN 1941,** when a third out was made, the players in the field did not bring their gloves with them into the dugout. First basemen and third basemen tossed their gloves into foul territory near their bases. Middle infielders threw their gloves into the middle of the diamond just off the infield dirt, and outfielders left their gloves on the outfield grass.

- **IN 1941,** there were no such things as ninth-inning closers. Nor were there seventh- and eighth-inning relievers known as setup pitchers. Starting pitchers were expected to go the distance. In 1941, Thornton Lee of the White Sox won the American League Most Complete Games Pitched title by hurling thirty complete games. (In 2021, the Yankees' Gerrit Cole won the same title by pitching two.)

- **IN 1941,** there was no such thing as analytics, the constant study of baseball statistics that has become a major factor in the decisions that baseball executives and managers make on and off the field.

Italy, many around the world suspected Japan might well have its sights set on the United States. Americans on the West Coast, sensing the same dangerous threat from across the Pacific as East Coasters had long been sensing from across the Atlantic, began preparing to shelter themselves from attack.

Amid such turmoil, it was hardly surprising that the United States bolstered its military forces. And it did so in a dramatic way. Convinced that an all-volunteer army would not adequately rebuild the one that had been steadily shrinking in size since the end of World War I, the government announced the first peacetime military draft in the nation's history.

The army had determined that it needed to call up and train 400,000 men in case the nation was drawn into the war. On October 16, 1940, every one of the nation's sixteen million men between the ages of twenty-one and thirty-five had to register for a draft lottery. Each person who registered

On September 7, 1940, the Germans' Luftwaffe attacked the city of London. Americans watched with rising dread as fighting beyond American shores continued to escalate.

Opposite page: Among the changes between 1941 and today are the streamlined, tight-fitting uniforms that replaced heavy, baggy woolen ones. Today's players have a host of specialized equipment as well, from high-tech sliding gloves on the hand of the base runner to the batting glove in the pocket of the player making the throw.

BASEBALL ON THE BRINK ◆ 9

would be given a number by his local draft board. Each man whose number was pulled at random had to show up for a year of war readiness training.

From the moment that the draft was announced, people wondered openly about what its effect on baseball would be. Throughout spring training, whenever a story about a major leaguer appeared in a newspaper or magazine, the player's draft status was sure to be given top billing. On March 8, 1941, Hugh "Losing Pitcher" Mulcahy of the Philadelphia Phillies became one of the first ballplayers called into service, accepting his fate with the exemplary announcement that he'd be joining a "winning team."

Then, on April 23, with the season underway, the second major leaguer got drafted. But this was no "Losing Pitcher." It was the Detroit Tigers' Hank

In the Pacific the war escalated as well. Here, Japanese troops celebrate the capture of the Chinese city of Nanjing.

Greenberg, one of baseball's superstars, one of the greatest sluggers the game had ever known. As novelist and essayist Stephen Hunter has written, "When [Greenberg] stood tall and straight at the plate, he appeared to be one of the gods of baseball." And he was. In the four seasons between 1937 and

PRESIDENT FRANKLIN D. ROOSEVELT TOOK TO THE RADIO TO GIVE ANOTHER OF WHAT HAD COME TO BE CALLED "FIRESIDE CHATS."

1940, Greenberg averaged 43 home runs and 148 runs batted in per year. In 1938, he had hit 58 homers, at that time the second most in a single season in the history of the major leagues. As the 1941 season began, Greenberg was coming off another banner year: he had led the Tigers to the American League pennant by hitting .340 with 41 home runs and 150 runs batted in, earning him his second Most Valuable Player Award. Fittingly, he was also the highest-paid player in all of baseball, and many believed he had a real chance of breaking one of the game's most revered records—Babe Ruth's career total of 714 home runs.

Hank Greenberg was admired for his on-field achievements and his principles alike: as the first great Jewish ballplayer, he practiced his faith by refusing to play on major Jewish holidays.

But only eight days after the 1940 World Series had ended with a Tigers' 2-1 loss to the Cincinnati Reds, Hank Greenberg made what he later called the greatest mistake of his life. After spending a few days cleaning out his locker and taking care of other chores, Greenberg joined his brother Joe (who was a minor league ballplayer) for the automobile ride from Detroit to the Bronx section of New York City where their parents lived. They set out on the morning of October 16, both of them aware it was the day that they, like millions of other American men, had to register for the draft.

THE MILITARY DRAFT

THE NATION'S FIRST PEACETIME MILITARY DRAFT, officially enacted by law as the Selective Training and Service Act of 1940, was held on October 29, 1940, and was based on a lottery system. In Washington, DC, the huge glass bowl that had been used for the same purpose in World War I was brought forth. The bowl was filled with small capsules, each containing a piece of paper upon which a number ranging from 1 to 7,836 had been printed.

Using a wooden spoon carved from a piece of Philadelphia's Independence Hall (where both the US Declaration of Independence and the US Constitution were adopted), draft officials vigorously stirred the contents of the bowl. Then, Secretary of War Henry Stimson, wearing a blindfold, reached into the bowl and pulled out a capsule. President Franklin Delano Roosevelt opened it and read out the number 158. In thousands of local draft districts across the United States, men who had been assigned that number had to report for service.

Before this draft, the US Army and Navy had a combined force of about 265,000. Within a month, more than sixteen million were on the draft rolls and almost a million had been drafted into military service.

The provisions of the act were clearly spelled out. Whomever was drafted was required to serve at least one year, plus up to ten years in the reserves. Although it was not supposed to be the case, the military remained segregated by race. White men who met all the requirements were drafted immediately. Particularly during the early period of the draft, draft boards sent most Black men home. Those few African Americans who were drafted were assigned to the very few all-Black military units that existed. Any draftee not meeting the medical requirements was classified as unfit for service (informally, "4-F") and was also sent home.

Men with wives and children were also exempt from service as were those engaged in "essential industries," farming, or attending college. Once the war began, and more and more men were needed in armed services, many of these exemptions were dropped.

A blindfolded United States Secretary of the Navy, Frank Knox, draws a conscription number to commence the first peacetime military draft.

When Hank and Joe stopped to register in the small town of Geneva, New York, Joe listed his parents' New York address as his home. Hank, on the other hand, gave his address as the hotel in Detroit where he lived during the baseball season. This turned out to be a huge error. In New York, even if he was drafted, his chances of getting a postponement, called a deferment, until the end of the 1941 baseball season would have been excellent. In Detroit, however, Greenberg was a huge sports hero, and constantly in the spotlight. The draft board, anxious to not be seen as favoring celebrities, would be unlikely to defer him if his number came up. As Greenberg told the press, "When you were called you went, and it didn't matter how famous you were. In fact, the more famous you were, the more attention was paid to you. Even if you had a good reason to seek a deferment, people didn't want to hear about it. They wanted you to serve, the same as their sons and brothers and cousins. No exceptions."

And sure enough, on April 23, number 621 was called. Greenberg was ordered to report for induction at 6:00 a.m. on May 7. His last game for the season was at Tiger Stadium against the Yankees where he said farewell by blasting two home runs. As author Mike Vaccaro has written, "While his [fellow ballplayers] would fill the coming months of 1941 with an astonishing array of accomplishments, Greenberg would be peeling potatoes in military kitchens, learning how to clean his rifle, and killing time in barracks with his fellow draftees, most of whom were ten or eleven years younger than him."

Unfortunately, things on the ever-widening warfront continued to get worse. So much so that even the ballfield could no longer remain an untouched respite from the bad news of the battlefield. Two months into the 1941 season, on the evening of May 27, in the Polo Grounds, the New York Giants were playing their first night game of the season against the Boston Braves (eleven of the sixteen major league stadiums now had lights) when the reality of war crashed straight into the middle of

Tigers superstar Hank Greenberg leaves the dugout, preparing to take the field for the final time before reporting for military service.

1941

	1941	2024
United States Population	133,417,000	336,419,000
United States Life Expectancy	Males: 63.1 years Females: 66.8 years	Males: 74.8 Females: 80.2 years
Average Annual Salary	$2,050	$59,384
Minimum Wage	30 cents/hour	$7.25/hour
Number of Farms in the United States	6 million	2 million

NEW PRODUCTS

- M&M's are invented as a means for soldiers to enjoy chocolate without it melting. During World War II (1941–1945), the candy is sold exclusively to the military.
- The breakfast cereal Cheerios is introduced as Cheerioats.

WHAT THINGS COST

ITEM	1941	2024
Average Cost of a House	$6,900	$416,100
Average Cost of a House Rental	$32/month	$2,100/month
Average Cost of a New Automobile	$825	$47,338
Gasoline	19 cents/gallon	$3.20/gallon
Postage Stamp	3 cents	73 cents
Cigarettes	12 cents/pack	$8/pack
Hershey Bar	5 cents	$1.79
Movie Ticket	25 cents	$10.78
Milk	34 cents/gallon	$4.05/gallon
Eggs	40 cents/dozen	$3.00/dozen
Coffee	24 cents/pound	$9.00/pound
Sugar	6 cents/pound	$1.00/pound
Bread	8 cents/pound	$2.55/loaf
Butter	41 cents/pound	$4.79/pound
Bacon	34 cents/pound	$6.79/pound
Round Steak	34 cents/pound	$9.29/pound

President Franklin Delano Roosevelt used radio broadcasts to keep the American people informed of the nation's response to global developments.

the baseball field. With the score tied at the end of the seventh inning, the umpires suddenly threw up their arms, stopping the game. As both teams left the field in bewilderment, the public address announcer informed the crowd that they were about to be tuned into a nationwide radio address by the president of the United States. The gravity of the situation was clear; never in the history of the major leagues had a game been interrupted for such a reason.

And there *was* a good reason for it. As circumstances continued driving the United States closer and closer to entering the war, President Roosevelt wanted the nation to pay attention to just how dire things were becoming.

England, the president stated, was in terrible trouble. Its homes, its cities, its factories, and its ports were under constant bombardment from German aircraft. The death toll from these attacks was staggering. On the European continent, the German Army had overrun Hungary, Romania, Bulgaria, and Yugoslavia, and had conquered Greece. Sadly, there was more. In the Atlantic, German submarines, called U-boats, were sinking British and American ships that were transporting supplies to England faster than these two nations could replace them. And in Africa, Roosevelt stated, Hitler's troops were fighting their way toward the strategically important Suez Canal.

The president then declared that the United States was now in a state of "unlimited national emergency." And then, in the most militant statement of his presidency to date, he continued, "We are placing our armed forces in strategic military position. We will not hesitate to use our armed forces to repel attack."

SOME EIGHTY-FIVE MILLION PEOPLE IN THE UNITED STATES LISTENED TO THE ADDRESS. THAT WAS MORE THAN HALF THE NATION'S POPULATION

Some eighty-five million people in the United States listened to the address. That was more than half the nation's population, the largest audience ever to listen to a radio broadcast in this country. National leaders had mixed reactions to it. New York's Mayor Fiorello LaGuardia called it "a statement the world will understand." Congressman Hamilton Fish, a passionate Roosevelt opponent, accused him of promoting "war hysteria." But whatever their position, all had to agree with former presidential candidate Alf Landon who pronounced that "the power is now in the President's hands . . . whether that means war is something else, but it does look like we're on our way."

At the Polo Grounds, the unprecedented forty-five-minute address was greeted with great applause. As soon as it ended, future Hall of Fame pitcher Carl Hubbell retook the mound and the game went on, and to the delight of the now late-staying home crowd, the Giants won.

2

THE STREAK

WHEN THE 1941 BASEBALL SEASON began, the New York Yankees were odds-on favorites to win the American League pennant. The "Bronx Bombers," as they were affectionately known, were a team of stars, including outfielders Tommy Henrich and Charlie Keller, second baseman Joe Gordon, catcher Bill Dickey, and pitchers Red Ruffing and Lefty Gomez. The greatest star of them all, however, was their twenty-six-year-old outfielder about to begin his sixth season with the team. His name was Joe DiMaggio.

Born in a small fishing village in California, DiMaggio was the eighth of nine children whose parents had immigrated to America from Italy. His fisherman father intended for Joe to follow in his footsteps, but like two of his brothers, Vince and Dominic, he showed an early, remarkable talent for baseball—so remarkable that he was only seventeen years old when he was signed by the New York Yankees and placed on the roster of their top minor league team, the San Francisco Seals of the Pacific Coast League.

And almost immediately, he caused a sensation. In his first full season with the Seals, he batted .340, hit twenty-eight home runs, and drove in 169 runs. Most spectacularly, he also hit safely in sixty-one straight games. During

Two baseball immortals square off in 1941. Hitter Joe DiMaggio and pitcher Bob Feller face each other in Cleveland.

the next two seasons, he continued to tear up the league, batting .341 and .398. And when he was called up to the Yankees at the beginning of the 1936 season, he quickly turned heads by batting .323, hitting twenty-nine homers, and knocking in 125 runs.

Quiet and serious-minded, DiMaggio was no attention seeker. He had certainly not seen himself as the replacement for Babe Ruth, the greatest Yankee of them all. But as the team's newest star, he was inevitably cast in that role. And there *was* one way in which he and Ruth were very much alike. Like Ruth, he was determined to be the very best. Toward the end of his career, a friend asked DiMaggio why, despite his age and the pain he often endured, he continued to play so hard. "Because," he responded, "there might

The Yankees lineup in 1941 included the all-star outfield of Joe DiMaggio, Charlie Keller, and Tommy Henrich, seen here with all-star second baseman Joe Gordon.

be somebody out there who's never seen me play before."

To see him play, either at bat or on the field, was invariably an unforgettable experience. At the plate, the man they called "the Yankee Clipper" was as graceful and efficient as in the outfield. "Joe DiMaggio batting," wrote the poet Donald Hall, "sometimes gave the . . . impression . . . that the old rules and dimensions of baseball no longer applied to him and that the game at last had grown unfairly easy." Casey Stengel, the Yankees' manager for DiMaggio's final three seasons, stated it simply: "He made the rest of them look like plumbers." His greatest hitting rival, Ted Williams, put it this way. "DiMaggio," Williams proclaimed, "even looks good striking out."

Not that he did that very often. During the entire 1941 season, DiMaggio fanned only thirteen times. There were other records, equally amazing. In one season, he made only one error in 141 games. In the course of his career, he threw out 153 base runners from the outfield. And that was not all. "He was the best base runner I ever saw," stated his longtime manager Joe McCarthy. "He could have stolen 50, 60 bases a year if I let him. He wasn't the fastest man alive, he just knew how to run bases better than anybody."

Joe DiMaggio, the twenty-seven-year old superstar, was about to do something that has never been done since. As baseball historian Michael Seidel has eloquently stated, "No other sustained performance in the history of baseball builds with the drama and explodes with the energy of Joe DiMaggio's 56-game consecutive hitting streak launched on a lazy Thursday afternoon in New York on May 15, 1941, and grounded on a damp summer night in Cleveland on July 17."

It began innocently enough. The 13-1 shellacking the Bronx Bombers took in Yankee Stadium at the hands of the Chicago White Sox on an oppressively hot May 15 afternoon marked their fifth loss in a row and their eighth

> A batting average tells how often a player gets a hit. A .300 average means the player got a hit 30 percent of the time they came up to the plate. A .200 average is poor, a .250 average is OK, and a .300 average is excellent. Averages above .300 are outstanding and not very common; only about fifteen players out of the five hundred batters in the major leagues hit above .300 every year.

A DIFFERENT WORLD

From April 14 to October 6, 1941, much of the United States remained enthralled in what was obviously a very special and shining Major League Baseball season. Meantime, much of the rest of the world was going through very different kinds of experiences. The following is a select list of but a few of the events that took place while Joe DiMaggio's immortal streak was unfolding:

MAY 21   The US merchant ship *Robin Moor* is sunk by a German submarine.

MAY 24   The British battle cruiser HMS *Hood* is sunk by the German battleship *Bismarck*.

MAY 27   The *Bismarck* is sunk in the North Atlantic by ships of the Royal Navy.

JUNE 22   Germany invades the Soviet Union with a three-pronged campaign called Operation Barbarossa aimed at Moscow, Leningrad, and Russian oil fields.

JUNE 25   The Soviet Union and Finland declare war on each other.

JUNE 27   Hungary and Slovakia declare war on the Soviet Union.

EARLY JULY   German troops carry out a mass murder of Polish scientists and writers in Poland.

in the last ten games. They were already five and a half games out of first place. DiMaggio, who throughout the first month of the season had been hitting over .500, was mired in a slump that had seen his batting average drop over two hundred points. The one hit he got off lefty Eddie Smith that day gave no indication that something quite incredible was about to follow.

The next day, the Yankees ended their losing streak, staging a ninth-inning rally to beat the White Sox 6-5. DiMaggio's long triple to left-center, his second hit of the day, was the key blow in the comeback. But it was his third-inning home run that fans would most remember. Blasted over the bullpen and deep into the bleacher seats in left field, it was the second-longest homer to left field that any American League ballplayer had ever hit in Yankee Stadium.

Two weeks later, on May 28, in the first night game ever played in

Opposite page: British Prime Minister Winston Churchill surveys bomb damage in the English city of Bristol.

Joe DiMaggio had one of the most powerful swings in baseball history.

Washington's Griffith Stadium, DiMaggio ran his hitting streak to thirteen straight games when he belted an eighth-inning triple. But his performance was vastly overshadowed by the news President Franklin D. Roosevelt had delivered the day before, when the contest at the Polo Grounds had been halted and the entire country stopped in its tracks to hear him announce the existence of an "unlimited national emergency."

The bad news would continue to come, but DiMaggio's play would continue to offer a bright spot all the same.

The second game of the Washington series was played under rainy skies that so swamped the field that the game was called off after five innings. That still made it an official contest, and fortunately DiMaggio had singled in the fourth inning, extending the streak to fourteen.

The next day in Boston for a Memorial Day doubleheader, DiMaggio drilled a sharp ninth-inning hit to help the Yankees come from behind and win the first game 4-3 of the second contest. At bat in the fifth inning, he got under a pitch and lifted a harmless fly ball to right field. But as the Red Sox's Pete Fox prepared to make an easy catch, he suddenly threw up his arms in frustration. He had lost sight of the ball in the sun. Since he had come nowhere near touching the ball, the official scorer had no choice but to rule it a hit. The streak was now at sixteen. And two days later, hits in both games of a doubleheader in Cleveland brought it to eighteen.

In Detroit on June 3, the same day that a national opinion poll revealed that a majority of Americans were in favor of sending war supplies to England, DiMaggio ran his streak to twenty. Two days later, he reached twenty-one with a triple off the Tigers' often "unhittable" hurler Hal Newhouser. On June 7, the same day that the wonder horse Whirlaway won the Belmont Stakes and became just the fifth winner of horseracing's Triple Crown, DiMaggio extended the streak to twenty-two. During the next day's doubleheader, he raised the mark to twenty-four.

He was now, he told one reporter, feeling more confident at the plate than at any time since the season began. But two days after his latest display

American citizens were proud to do their part in supporting the Allies, as seen here celebrating the dedication of an armor plate factory for defense purposes.

> A player gets a hit if he hits a fair ball where there's no realistic chance it can be fielded cleanly. If the fielder does have a chance to field a batted ball, but bungles the attempt to catch or field it, that's an error and the batter does not get credit for a hit.

of power, DiMaggio once again needed a dose of good fortune to keep the streak alive. Facing the White Sox in Chicago, he came to bat in the seventh inning in what, in all probability, would be his final trip to the plate. Standing in against White Sox–ace Johnny Rigney, who had blanked him thus far, DiMaggio smashed a viciously hit ground ball directly at slick-fielding third-baseman Dario Lodigiani, who twice before during the season had robbed him of hits. This time, the hard smash handcuffed the infielder and skipped away from him. Was it an error (which would not count as a hit)? Was the streak still alive or was it dead? Unlike today, there was no replay with officials looking at tape of what had happened from every possible angle. After what seemed like forever, the scorer made his decision. The ball was too hard-hit for Lodigiani to handle, he ruled. It was a hit. The streak was still alive.

The next two games provided no such suspense. Delivering base hits early on in each game, DiMaggio extended the streak to twenty-eight—one game away from tying the Yankees all-time hitting-streak record set by Roger Peckinpaugh in 1919 and equaled by Earle Combs in 1931.

On June 16, global relations had deteriorated to the point that the United States ordered all German and Italian government officials in the country to close down their embassies and return home. That same day, fans streamed into Yankee Stadium hoping for a respite from bad news, and hoping to see DiMaggio match the long-standing Yankee hitting-streak record.

What no one had hoped for was the rain that caused an hour and a half delay in the game. Those who sat through the long delay, however, were rewarded when, in the fifth inning, with the crowd cheering his every move, DiMaggio belted a double to left to tie the mark.

It was not only a triumph for the man of the hour but for his team as well. By beating the Indians 6-4, the Yankees completed a sweep of the three-game series and now trailed league-leading Cleveland by just one game. DiMaggio's streak was not only a personal victory but a significant factor in the pennant race as well.

The next day, DiMaggio would be attempting to break the all-time Yankee record in a game with the Chicago White Sox, the same team against whom he had begun his streak. Late in the game, he was still hitless, and, in the press box, more than one reporter was preparing to write about how disappointing it was that the great streak had ended one hit short of a new Yankee record. But in the seventh inning, DiMaggio hit a vicious ground ball that took a crazy hop, struck shortstop Luke Appling on the shoulder, and bounced into left field. The Yankee Stadium crowd held its breath waiting for yet another official scorer to make yet another fateful decision. After what seemed like an eternity, he ruled it a hit. A new Yankee hitting-streak record of thirty straight games had been set.

As author Lew Freedman has written, "It didn't hurt any that DiMaggio played for a team located in the heart of the media center of the United States and that New York newspapers competed to one-up one another with

IT WAS NOT ONLY A TRIUMPH FOR THE MAN OF THE HOUR BUT FOR HIS TEAM AS WELL.

every scrap of news." And now that the streak had reached thirty, news about it became a national obsession. In his book *Baseball in '41*, author Robert Creamer shared the story of how, in the summer of 1941, one of his friends drove across the United States in an old car. "In Montana," Creamer wrote, "[he] stopped for coffee at a dusty café in a dusty town. Farmhands and ranch hands came into the café for breakfast. This was before television . . . and radio news was sketchy before we got into the war, particularly in smaller towns. You found out what was happening from newspapers. Almost every

Although he hid it well, the streak was a nerve-racking experience for DiMaggio.

man who came into the café, [the friend said,] would ask the proprietor, 'he get one yesterday?' He didn't have to explain who 'he' was, even though this was 2000 miles from New York and 1000 miles west of the western-most major league city, which in those days was St. Louis. Every day, all over the country, people asked 'did he get one yesterday?'"

Every day, the United States seemed to be drawing closer and closer to global war. Yet, millions of people were increasingly focused on that day's (or night's) Yankees' game. Soon radio stations began interrupting even their most popular programs with bulletins announcing DiMaggio's streak-extending hit.

And soon there was a song, extolling DiMaggio and his streak and endowing him with a new nickname. Written by Alan Courtney and Ben Homer, it was titled "Joltin' Joe DiMaggio."

At one of the most anxious times in its history, the nation welcomed the chance to cheer for a ballplayer to keep doing what he did best. As *Sports Illustrated*'s Dave Anderson wrote, "For the fans there was no escape from the magnetic force that drew them to their radios to hear the news announcer report the grim but still dreamlike news of the war in Europe, and then, at some point in the program, add, 'and Joe DiMaggio got his hit today.'"

As the streak continued and the pressure to keep it alive mounted, those closest to DiMaggio marveled at how calm he appeared to be through it all—calmer, it seemed, than his fans and teammates. Not until the season was over did he reveal what a misconception that was: how he was having great trouble sleeping, how he had developed ulcers, and how increasingly in games when he had not yet had a hit, he found himself pacing beneath the stands smoking one cigarette after another. "I was able to control myself," he later stated, "but that doesn't mean that I wasn't dying inside."

On June 18, with the sports world abuzz over the heavyweight championship fight that was to take place between Joe Louis and Billy Conn, DiMaggio extended the streak to thirty-one. The next game, DiMaggio hit a single in the first inning.

Two days later, the Yankees staged a first-inning hitting barrage against the Tigers' Bobo Newsom, including a DiMaggio single that quickly set the streak at thirty-three. Before the game was over, he contributed two more singles and a double to the final 14-4 score.

Most important, as DiMaggio himself later confirmed, his two-day batting spree convinced him to set his sights higher still. For the first time, he believed he had a real chance of breaking two other consecutive-game hitting streak records, records that were even longer and more highly regarded than the Yankees' record that he had just shattered, records that had long been regarded as unbreakable. The first of these was the American League mark of forty-one straight games set in 1922 by Hall of Fame first baseman George Sisler. The other was the Major League Baseball record of forty-four straight games set by Hall of Fame outfielder "Wee Willie" Keeler in 1897.

On June 21, DiMaggio blooped a first-inning single over the head of Tigers' first baseman, Rudy York. He had mustered a first-inning hit in each of his past three games and had tallied eight hits in a row over those last three games.

Many of the fans arriving at the ballpark on June 22 had more than baseball on their minds. That morning, an enormous German army had invaded Russia, the massive country that had begun the European war as an ally of Germany and Italy before abruptly changing sides. A German victory over Russia, almost everyone knew, would be the most disastrous news yet to come out of the growing conflict. On this day, as had been happening for more than a month, DiMaggio's streak proved a compelling distraction. It was not until the sixth inning that he extended the streak to thirty-five by belting a homer off Tigers' ace Hal Newhouser. With this blast, the Yankees also set a new team consecutive-game home run record at eighteen.

On June 25, George Sisler's "unobtainable" forty-one-straight game record looked more attainable than ever when, against the Browns, DiMaggio raised his streak to thirty-seven by drilling a two-run fourth-inning homer into Yankee Stadium's left field seats. Sisler's mark was only four games away.

NOT SINCE THE STREAK HAD BEGUN HAD IT BEEN IN SUCH PERIL.

And the next day provided what one journalist called "the most exciting, electric moment of DiMaggio's hitting streak thus far." In the second inning, DiMaggio swung at a 3-0 pitch and flied out to left field. In the fourth, he reached base on an error by the Browns' shortstop—another at bat without registering a hit. He came up to the plate again in the sixth and was retired on an easy grounder to third. Not since the streak had begun had it been in such peril. The Yankees were ahead in the game 3-1, and if they stayed in the lead, they would not come to bat in the ninth.

In the bottom of the eighth, the score was still 3-1, and with the way pitcher Marius Russo had been mowing the Browns down all game, few doubted that this would be the Bronx Bombers' last time at the plate. DiMaggio was due up fourth in the inning; if none of the three batters ahead of him got on base, the streak was over.

Johnny Sturm led off—and popped out. With the crowd pleading with Red Rolfe to get on and give DiMaggio a final chance, the Yankees' third baseman worked the Browns' pitcher Elden Auker for a walk. Tommy Henrich was next, and he was deeply troubled. What if he hit into an inning-ending double play? DiMaggio's day at the plate would be over. And so would the streak.

Just as he was about to step into the batter's box, Henrich suddenly turned and headed back to the dugout. He had an idea, but to carry it out, he needed approval from Yankee manager Joe McCarthy. Although it was a highly unusual thing to do with a two-run lead in the eighth inning, he was thinking of laying down a bunt. That way, he could all but eliminate the chance of a double play. McCarthy, anxious to give DiMaggio a final chance, approved the plan. And after Henrich laid down a perfect bunt, Rolfe stood safely at second with DiMaggio striding to the plate.

The tension in Yankee Stadium could not have been greater. Mercifully, neither those in the stands nor those glued to their radios had to suffer long. Swinging at Auker's first pitch, DiMaggio drove it on a line past the third baseman and into the left field corner for a run-scoring double. The streak lived on!

The stadium crowd responded by cheering themselves hoarse. DiMaggio's teammates had their own special reaction. "When DiMaggio finally got his hit," wrote one reporter, "the Yankees rushed out on the field and put on a bigger demonstration than their 1927 predecessors did when Babe Ruth hit his 60th homer and the all-time mark."

The next day's game in Philadelphia was far less dramatic. DiMaggio made sure of that in the first inning, hitting the first pitch

The streak was covered widely in newspapers across the country. This was the *Detroit Evening Times* of June 26, 1941.

ANOTHER REMARKABLE RECORD

On June 1, 1941, during the second game of a doubleheader in Cleveland's Municipal Stadium, Joe DiMaggio extended his consecutive-game hitting streak to eighteen games. In that game, the Yankees' first baseman was the much lesser-known Johnny Sturm. He was, in fact, the Yankees' first baseman for the entire season, having replaced Babe Dahlgren, the man who had taken over for Lou Gehrig when the Yankee legend was forced to step down after playing in a then record 2,130 games. Sturm batted only .239 for the season and hit only three home runs. But the first of these round-trippers came in the second game of the doubleheader and was a far more momentous blast than anyone at the time could have imagined.

Sturm's round-tripper was the beginning of a streak in which the Yankees, from June 1 to June 29, hit a home run in twenty-five straight games. It was a consecutive-game team home run record that would last for fifty-three years. It was also a streak that fans around the country followed closely until it was overshadowed by DiMaggio's historic run.

The record was finally broken more than fifty years later, when the 2002 Texas Rangers, with Alex Rodriguez, Rafael Palmero, and Ivan Rodriguez leading the way, hit home runs in twenty-seven straight games.

In 2019, the Yankees reclaimed the record with one of the greatest demonstrations of power hitting in baseball history. Beginning with the second game of a doubleheader against the Kansas City Royals, on May 25, the Yankees hit at least one home run in thirty-one consecutive games. During that streak, the Bronx Bombers belted fifty-seven round-trippers with fourteen different players hitting home runs. Gary Sanchez and DJ LeMahieu led the way, each blasting eight homers during the streak, which was finally stopped on July 3, 2019, by the Yankees' crosstown rivals, the New York Mets.

thrown to him into center field for a clean single. When he blasted a homer deep to left in the seventh, he took over the American League home run lead with seventeen.

But another challenging game was on the horizon the following day against the formidable A's pitcher Johnny Babich. Last season, he had beaten the Bronx Bombers an unheard-of five times. Now, with the streak at thirty-nine, two games shy of Sisler's coveted record, Babich pledged he would be the pitcher who put an end to it. He was determined to do it, he said, even if it meant defying his manager's orders to give DiMaggio a fair chance. The Yankees' slugger, Babich boasted, was not going to get a single pitch in the strike zone to hit.

He was true to his word. During his first time at bat, DiMaggio did not see anything worth swinging at, and the first three pitches that Babich threw to him in the fourth were more of the same. With the count 3-0, the hometown Philadelphia crowd began to boo their own pitcher. It didn't faze Babich. His next pitch was clearly outside, intended to be ball four. But DiMaggio reached across the plate and slammed it on a line into right center field for a double. Later, when he was asked which hits during the streak pleased him most, this was always one of the first that he mentioned.

On June 29, the front pages of the nation's newspapers were filled with attention-grabbing stories: There had been an enormous increase in fighter and bomber plane production, and there was a new military draft call-up of 900,000 men.

There was very little joy anywhere within the publications. With one glaring exception. The largest headline of all was reserved for the announcement that in a doubleheader that day, in the Washington Senators' ballpark, Joe DiMaggio would be attempting to tie and then break George Sisler's legendary hitting-streak record.

It was a tense day, and it was hot—over a hundred degrees. In his first time at bat in the first game, DiMaggio hit a scalding line drive, but it was hauled down by the Senators' center fielder. On his second time at the plate, he

On June 30, 1941, DiMaggio broke George Sisler's long-standing consecutive game hitting streak.

went after a 3-0 pitch and popped out to third base. In the sixth inning, knuckleball pitcher Dutch Leonard tried to slip a fastball past him, but the trick didn't work. Somehow guessing what Leonard was up to, DiMaggio slammed a line drive to left center that rolled more than 420 feet to the wall. The Yankees' bench, their bullpen, and the ecstatic crowd erupted into a prolonged roar. Sisler's record had been tied.

Would it be broken in the second game? It sure didn't look that way when DiMaggio came to bat in the seventh inning for probably the last time, having made three routine outs in his previous plate appearances. But after ducking back from a fastball up around his chin, he drove the next pitch into left field for a clean single. Joe DiMaggio now held the American League consecutive-game hitting record at forty-two. As the crowd erupted for the second time that day, the entire Yankees' dugout scrambled to the top of the steps where, according to *The Washington Post*, they performed "their version of a jig."

If Americans needed a reminder that the world situation was not getting any better, it came with the announcement by the US government on July 1 of a second registration for the draft, targeting men who had turned twenty-one in the past eight months. At the same time, baseball fans and the insatiable sports press were aware that another record loomed large: "Wee Willy" Keeler's Major League Baseball (MLB) hitting-streak record of forty-four games, set in 1897. Once again, the challenge would come during a doubleheader, this one at home against the archrival Boston Red Sox. Despite temperatures that rose to ninety-five degrees, almost 53,000 fans poured into Yankee Stadium hoping to see their hero tie Keeler's record.

In the first game, enormous cheers broke out each time DiMaggio stepped to the plate. But after two times at bat, he remained hitless. Then in the fifth, he hit a hard grounder to third that handcuffed the Red Sox's third baseman. Once again, as had happened so often during the streak, the huge crowd could only nervously wait until the official scorer made his decision. Then finally it came. It was a hit! Keeler's MLB record was one game away. The second game of the twin bill was far less dramatic. In the bottom of the first, DiMaggio lined a single over shortstop Joe Cronin's head. The MLB record, set before the turn of the century, had been tied.

The next day, the potential record-breaking day, was, if anything, even hotter. So hot that the Red Sox decided to replace their aging starting pitcher, the veteran star Lefty Grove, with rookie Dick Newsome. And for the second straight day it seemed that DiMaggio would end the tension quickly. In his first at bat, he hit a long drive to right that seemed destined to be the record breaker. But, after a long run, right fielder Stan Spence snared it with a leaping catch. The second time up, DiMaggio hit the ball even harder to the deepest part of center field. But once again he was thwarted by an

DiMaggio's managers, coaches, and teammates were overwhelmingly caught up in the streak.

Along with his hitting and fielding skills, DiMaggio was one of major league baseball's most accomplished base runners.

even more spectacular grab—by his own brother. "It was a great catch," DiMaggio said after the game. "It was one of the best Dom ever made, but at that moment the only thing on my mind was the temptation to withdraw the dinner invitation I had extended to [him]."

In his third trip to the plate, DiMaggio refused to be robbed again. On a 2 and 1 pitch, with two men on base, he lined a "rocket" well into the left field stands. As he rounded the bases, bedlam erupted. Even the reporters in the press box were on their feet cheering the man who had broken a record that for so long seemed unbreakable.

He was far from done. With the pressure off, he actually began hitting better than ever. On July 11 in St. Louis, the streak reached fifty, and a July 16 rout of the second-place Indians brought the streak to fifty-six.

The next day, 67,468 people, the largest crowd of the 1941 season, made their way into Cleveland's Municipal Stadium to witness DiMaggio's attempt to extend the streak and to watch what might be the Indians' last chance to make a serious run at the now league-leading Yankees. On his first turn at bat, DiMaggio hit a hard shot down the third baseline, a smash that seemed certain to be a base hit. But Ken Keltner, widely regarded as the best third baseman in the American League, was ready to meet it. Keltner backhanded DiMaggio's blast and threw a "rope" to first, nailing the Yankee Clipper by an eyelash.

When Cleveland hurler Al Smith walked DiMaggio the next time he came up, the huge stadium was racked with boos. The fans wanted their

Indians to win, but they also wanted the Yankees' star to continue the magical streak that they had been following for more than two months.

DiMaggio came up again in the seventh, and the result was a carbon copy of what had happened in the first. Again he hit a smash along the third base line that seemed headed for left field. Again Keltner made a great snag of the ball, and again he threw DiMaggio out by less than a step. Once more, it seemed, it would all come down to a last time at bat. Thanks to a Yankee rally, that came in the eighth. With most of the more than 67,000 spectators either standing or sitting on the edge of their seats, the man who so many times had saved the streak on his last turn at bat hit a routine grounder to the shortstop that resulted in a double play. But all hope was not yet lost: The Indians were trailing 4-3 going into the ninth. And when the Indians' Larry Rosenthal hit a booming triple with no one out, extra innings—and another DiMaggio turn at the plate—seemed all but assured. But it was not meant

On July 16, 1941, DiMaggio hit safely in his fifty-sixth straight game.

to be. The next three Cleveland batters went out without scoring a run. The streak was officially over.

Having robbed the baseball world of one of its most fervent pastimes—following the streak—Ken Keltner, for his own safety, was escorted out of the ballpark by police. An absolutely exhausted Joe DiMaggio went out to dinner alone, too drained to talk with anyone.

A key to Joe DiMaggio's greatness was his impeccable attention to details. Here he prepares his bat before a game.

But he was back in the lineup the next day. And he immediately began another streak, hitting safely in sixteen straight games. That meant that from the middle of May until the beginning of August, he had a base hit in an amazing seventy-two out of seventy-three games. Even more astounding were the statistics that he compiled during the streak. Between May 15 and July 16, he came to bat 223 times and pounded out ninety-one hits for a .408 batting average. He hit fifty-six singles, sixteen doubles, four triples, and fifteen home runs. He knocked in fifty-five runs and scored fifty-six runs. Through it all, he struck out only seven times.

Just as remarkable was what the streak did for the Yankees. DiMaggio's fellow outfielder Tommy Henrich was particularly vocal about how Joltin' Joe's streak turned the Yankees' season around. Referring to the Yankees' record of 14-15 before the streak began, Henrich stated, "We weren't playing well at all. The Yankees didn't usually occupy that neighborhood in those days. That was all right if you were used to finishing in the middle of the pack, but we were the Yankees. We knew we were better than that. After our third-place finish of the year before, we knew we had to get hot. We did, and Joe D., the 'Yankee Clipper,' was the one who ignited our fire."

"Ignited" was much too mild a word. During the streak, the Yankees won forty-one games while losing only nineteen (there were two ties because of rainstorms). When the streak began, the Bronx Bombers were in fourth place in the American League. When it ended, they were seven games in front.

When DiMaggio's record hitting streak ended, he was surrounded by his teammates and his manager, Joe McCarthy, all anxious to show their admiration for his record-breaking performance and what it had contributed to their 1941 season.

Joe DiMaggio's historic streak officially ended on July 17, 1941, two days after a British scientific report concluded that the making of an atomic bomb was possible and was "likely to lead to decisive results in the war." But, in many ways, the streak has never died. It remains in the memory of all who cherish great accomplishments. The streak, Robert Creamer wrote, "[went beyond] baseball. Everyone was caught up in it. No athlete before or since—not Babe Ruth or Jack Dempsey or Bobby Jones; not Jackie Robinson or Mary Lou Retton; not Mohammed Ali . . . has held the country's fascinated attention day after day, week after week, the way DiMaggio did in 1941." Lou Boudreau, the great manager and shortstop of the Cleveland Indians, put it simply. "To me," he said, "it was the greatest thing that's ever happened in baseball."

DiMaggio's feat is prominently featured on his Baseball Hall of Fame plaque.

THE STREAK ♦ 41

3

THE KID

WITH THE GREAT STREAK OVER in mid-July, the attention of the baseball world turned to a tall, skinny twenty-three-year-old Red Sox outfielder who, throughout DiMaggio's march to glory, had actually been hitting at a higher clip than the Yankee star. His name was Ted Williams, and in this, his third year in the majors, he was making a serious run at an entirely different record: reaching a .400 batting average over the course of a full season. To achieve that extraordinary goal, a hitter had to average two hits in every five turns at bat. Even superior hitters like DiMaggio or the National League's Mel Ott proved unable to maintain such a pace over what was then a 154-game season against so many powerhouse pitchers. But by the time DiMaggio's magical consecutive-game hitting streak ended, many of those close to the game were beginning to believe that this brash youngster with the picture-perfect swing just might have a chance to do it.

Even in his schoolboy days, Williams had shown a remarkable talent at the plate. "My, he could hit 'em high," remembered one of his schoolmates. "Far OK, but high was the thing," he added. "That is why we [rode our bikes to] wherever he played. We wanted Williams to hit one and we just squealed when he

In 1942, along with Joe DiMaggio, the American League would be graced with another all-time hitting great—the Red Sox's Ted Williams.

From the moment he entered the minor leagues, Williams, shown here with the Minneapolis Millers of the American Association, demonstrated that he was destined to become a superstar.

put it so far up in the air and then so far out of the park."

Williams was still in high school when he started attracting big-league scouts and, like DiMaggio, was only seventeen when he began playing in the Pacific Coast League, for the San Diego Padres. Two years later, the Red Sox promoted him to their top farm club, the Minneapolis Millers. Fortunately for the young prospect, the Millers' batting coach was the legendary Rogers Hornsby, one of the greatest hitters ever to play the game. Hornsby taught Williams a simple but valuable batting rule: "Get a good pitch to hit." Under Hornsby's tutelage, Williams became, in the words of one baseball scribe, "perhaps the most single-minded student of hitting ever to play professional baseball."

He was still only nineteen when the Red Sox brought him up to the majors. Six feet, three inches tall and thin as a rail, he'd immediately been given a host of nicknames by the sports writers—"Toothpick Ted," "Willowy Walloper," "String Bean Slugger." The one that stuck was "Splendid Splinter." The one he liked best was "the Kid." During his first two years with the Red Sox, he was inarguably a really good ballplayer. But no one was yet ready to call him a great one. First of all, as good a hitter as he was, he was a mediocre outfielder, and visibly uninterested in getting any better at it. Secondly, he had a behavior problem, and was prone to temper tantrums, sometimes throwing his bat toward the dugout after striking out, or kicking the watercooler when things didn't go his way. Jimmie Foxx, the Red Sox's hard-hitting first baseman, called him a "spoiled kid." Another teammate described him as a "great hitter, but he could be a lot greater if someone would just spank his fanny."

It did not take the Boston crowd long to sour on him. Instead of ignoring the fans' taunts and catcalls, he yelled equally unkind things back at them. Worst of all as far as the fans were concerned, he refused to follow a time-honored baseball tradition of tipping his cap to the crowd to acknowledge their cheers after he hit a home run or after he came through with a crucial hit.

As cantankerous as his relationship with the Fenway fans was, his relationship with the Boston press was even worse. There were dozens of newspapers in the city, each one trying to outdo the others with attention-grabbing stories, and they climbed all over the young star, exaggerating every negative thing he did, often minimizing the good or great things he accomplished. Bill Cunningham was one of the Boston sportswriters with whom Williams had a running feud. But even he had to admit that Williams took "as brutal and as cruel a cuffing from some elements from the sports press as a kid was ever called upon to suffer. Maybe from our way of looking at it he asked for it, but whether he asked for it or not he got it and there was never anything quite like it."

Williams's reaction to the abuse he took his first two years was simple: he told a reporter that he wanted to be traded. "I do not like the town," he exclaimed. "I don't like the people and the town and the newspaper men have been on my back . . . I want to get out of town, and I am praying they trade me."

Ted Williams's rookie baseball card has become one of the most valuable in baseball history.

Nowadays, Williams would not have had to pray to be traded. The modern established practice of free agency would have allowed him, after six years of playing for the Red Sox, to sell his services to any other team he wished to join. But in the 1940s, players' contracts had no such option. Besides, as far as the Red Sox were concerned, how do you trade someone who could hit like Ted Williams? In his rookie year, he batted .327 and led the league in runs batted in. The next season, he hit .344. With such a promising start, who knew how high he might be able to bat in 1941? Did anyone dare even think about the seemingly impossible .400 mark?

Perhaps more than anyone who had ever played the game, Ted Williams was obsessed with hitting. "In order to do the toughest thing there is to do in sport—hit a baseball properly," he said, "a man has got to devote every ounce of his concentration to it." And concentrate he did. He not only thought and talked hitting; he breathed it as well. He constantly squeezed a rubber ball to strengthen his grip. He refused to drink alcohol. And he was meticulous

Pitchers' struggles to get Williams out led to the Williams Shift, the forerunner to the fielder's shift that was a key part of baseball strategy in the 2010s.

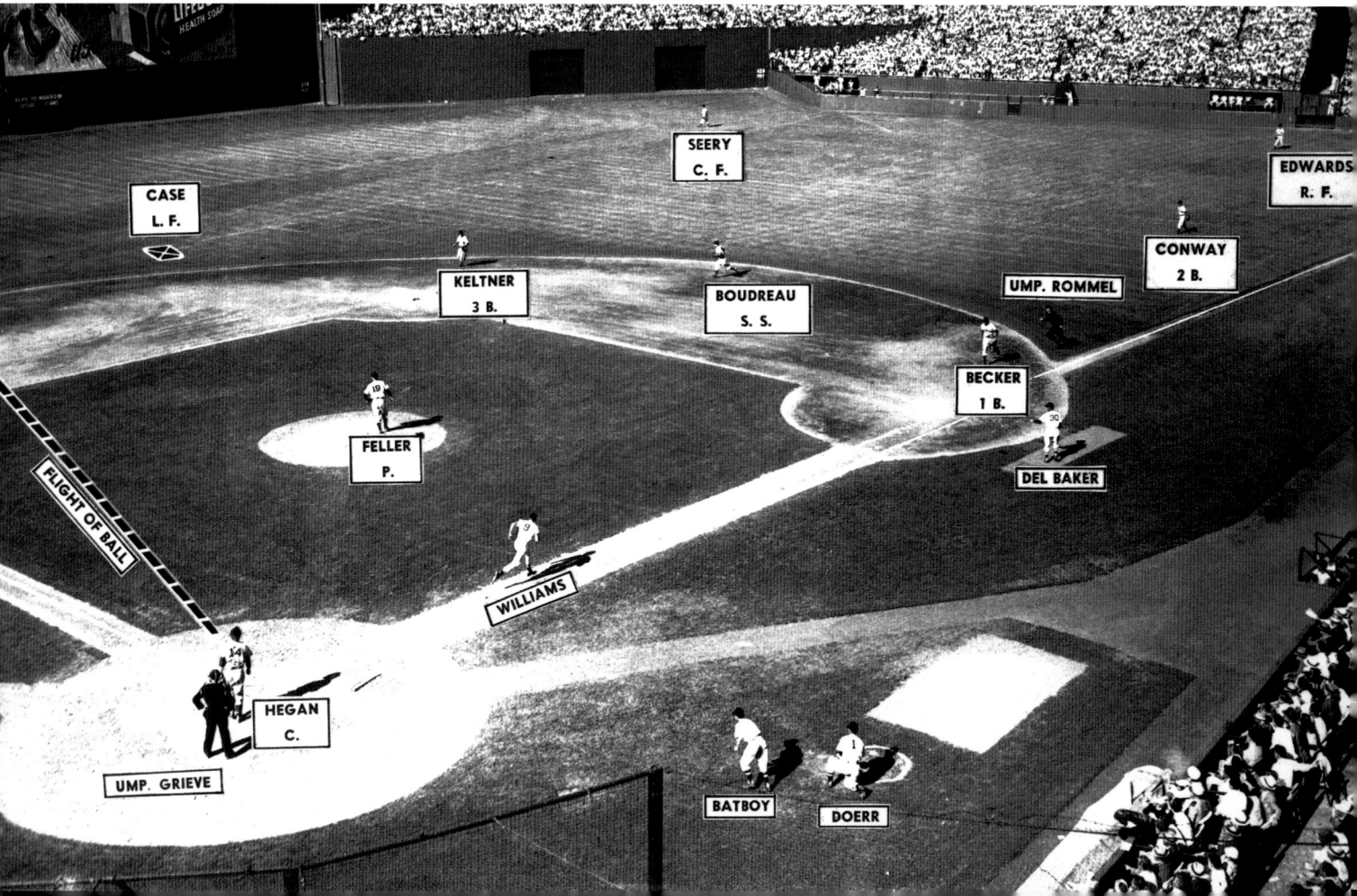

By the time the 1941 season was over Ted Williams would be regarded as perhaps the best pure hitter baseball had ever known.

about his equipment. "I always used lighter bats, usually 33 or 34 ounces, never more than 34, sometimes as light as 31. Then in the earlier part of the year I'd go with a heavier one, with better wood. You are stronger then, the pitchers are working to get their stuff down to get their control. I always worked with my bats, honing them down, putting a shine on them, forcing the fibers together. I treated them like babies. Weight tolerance got to be a big thing with me. The weight can change. Early in the season it's cold and damp and the bats lying on the ground pick up moisture and get heavier. I used to take them down to the post office to have them weighed."

This extraordinary attention to detail did not stop with his bats. "A trip to the plate was an adventure for me, one that I could reflect on and store up information," he wrote in his autobiography. "I honestly believe I can recall everything there was to know about my first three hundred home runs—who the pitcher was, the count, the pitch itself, where the ball landed. I did not have to keep a written book on pitchers—I lived a book on pitchers. I was a guy who practiced until the blisters bled and then practiced some more. When I was a kid I carried my bat to class with me, I would run a buddy's newspaper route if I could get him to shag flies for me. When I played for the San Diego Padres, I paid kids to shag flies on my days off."

The legendary Babe Ruth was among the first to predict that Williams would set baseball-batting records that might never be broken.

Opposite page: Even with Joe DiMaggio's amazing streak, there was real debate whether he or Ted Williams would win the 1941 American League batting championship.

Perhaps then it's not a total surprise that, early in the 1941 season, after he watched Williams play, Babe Ruth told reporters that the young man had a chance to hit .400. "A baseball comes at you too fast to begin thinking about it only after it leaves the pitcher's hand," Ruth explained. "Most hitters cheat by timing a back swing to pick up the rhythm of a pitcher's motion. The reason my own number 3 was so visible on my back directly from center field was that I exaggerated my back swing before the pitcher's release. But Williams waits much longer. The strength of his wrists, the speed of his swing and the uncoiling of his hips are exceptional. He gets a better look and a better cut. Yeah, he could do it, he could hit .400."

It was an exceptional statement, particularly coming from the great Babe Ruth. But in mid-May, the prediction seemed unfounded. At this point Williams was hitting .333. A reputable average for sure, but nowhere in the neighborhood of .400. Then he got red hot. A day before Joe DiMaggio began his historic streak, Williams started one of his own, hitting safely in twenty-three games before being shut out in a doubleheader in Chicago. More remarkably, he had thirty-six hits in fifty-six times at bat. His batting average climbed forty points in one week, and continued to soar. On May 30, as news of the strengthening alliance between Japan and Germany brought further anxiety to peace-loving people around the globe, Williams pounded out six hits in a doubleheader and was now hitting .429. Two days later, in another doubleheader, he went four for nine. On June 6, he reached a season high: .436. "It's a dream I've always had, the way I'm hitting now," he told a reporter. "Boy, I'm just busting the cover off that ball. I'm lucky because a lot of my drives are going where [the fielders] ain't. [But] hell, it's only June. I may be down to .360 in another month."

And his prediction soon seemed like prophecy, as he went into a sudden

Williams May Beat DiMaggio For Title

When Joe Breaks Record, He Pulverizes It

By DAN PARKER

WHEN JOE DiMAGGIO BREAKS a record, he doesn't stop at a mere fracture. He pulverizes it.

On the dot of 4:10 p. m. (E.D.T.), in a sweltering Yankee Stadium, Wednesday afternoon, the swatting Sicilian, twice the victim of dazzling bits of fielding in two previous trips to the plate, poled a homer into the lower tier of the left field grandstand, shattering the 44-year-old record of Wee Willie Keeler and establishing an all-time major league standard of hitting safely in 45 consecutive games. The record-breaking homer, made in the fifth inning with one out and Red Rolfe on second, was Joe's 100th hit of the season and his 18th homer. A comparatively small crowd of 8,682 saw this brilliant new chapter of baseball history written, but to the gate Je an ovation worthy of the vast assemblage that saw him tie Keeler's mark of 44 games the day before.

Having broken every existing major league record for hitting in consecutive games since he passed George Sisler's modern mark Sunday in Washington, DiMaggio now has two minor league records at which to shoot. The first is his own, set in 1933 in the Pacific Coast League, when he hit in 61 games in succession. If Joe passes that, there'll still be Joe Wilhoit's minor league mark of 69 games to surpass, made in 1919 with Wichita of the Western League.

And if anyone digs up any other records along the same line, Jolting Giuseppe will take care of them, too.

The whole country was waiting breathlessly Wednesday afternoon for news on DiMaggio, in decided contrast to what happened in 1897 when Keeler set his record. Radio hadn't even been dreamed of in that day, and the newspapers dismissed Wee Willie's feat with a line or two at the bottom of the baseball stories.

Watching Joe erase Keeler's record from the books was Tommy Connolly, supervisor of umpires in the American League. Tommy saw both Bad Bill Dahlen and Keeler run up their strings. Tommy paid Joe the biggest compliment a member of his profession can give a ball player when he talked to him after the game.

"Keeler was just like you, Joe," said the venerable dean of umpires. "He never looked back at an umpire"

Another thing Joe hardly ever does is strike out. Almost every ball he connects with is a poli.ciful base hit. Twice Wednesday, before he finally came through with his record-breaking homer, he had base hits snatched out of his grasp by larcenous Red Sox fielders. In the first inning, Spence happened to be playing Joe right and thus was able to make a leaping catch of his liner to right center after a hard run. In the third, Joe smashed a grass cutter along the third base line that Tabor snared with a back-hand stab just inside the base.

Heber Newsome, pitching for the Red Sox and hoping to win the glory of stopping DiMaggio, fed him two bad ones when he came up in the fifth with one out and Red Rolfe on second. The next pitch Joe leaned on with all his Sicilian sinew and poled it into the top tier of the left fields (and, a few yards outside the foul line. This was prophetic. Joe had the range. On the next toss, he smashed a cloud grazer out to left that cleared the barrier by 20 or 30 feet.

Mrs. DiMaggio, sitting tensely near the Yankee dugout, leaped out of her seat and uttered a cry of joy, drowned in the ocean of applause that marked the shattering of a record that had endured since the year before the Spanish-American War. Even in the blase press box, some of the boys forgot that studied nonchalance and gave with substantial yells. It was indeed a memorable moment.

Joe, who takes everything in stride, is upset more by the by-products of his hitting streak than by worry that it is going to be stopped. He is being deluged with fan mail, telegrams, phone calls and personal greetings. A quiet guy who likes the serenity of routine existence, Joe finds all this a bit disturbing—so much so that he hasn't opened any of his wires or mail yet.

After breaking the record, he asked Lefty Gomez, his pal: "When are we going to have another picnic?" On a recent Monday, he and his wife, Lefty and his wife and baby, and Paul Purdy, the bat boy, his wife and children, went on an old-fashioned picnic at Bear Mountain, and his wife seems to have enjoyed it even more than the kids. It didn't occur to him Wednesday that he's having a picnic all by himself with those rival pitchers.

For a guy who wasn't interested in baseball as a young lad but wanted to be a star tennis player, and also for a ball player whose price tag was cut from $75,000 to $25,000 plus a few pieces of ivory when he developed a trick knee in San Francisco, Giuseppe DiMaggio is doing all right.

(Copyright, 1941, King Features Syndicate)

THE BOX SCORE

```
GIANTS
(First game)       ab r h rbi po a
J. Moore, lf        ...
Rucker, rf          ...
Orengo, 2b          ...
Ott, rf             ...
O'Dea, c            ...
Carpenter, 2b       ...
Adams, p            ...
Danning, c          ...
Witek, ss           ...
Totals             43  4  8 24 10

BRAVES
                   ab r h o a
Sisti, 3b           ...
Cooney, cf          ...
Hassett, 1b         ...
West, lf            ...
Waner, rf           ...
Rowell, 2b          ...
Miller, ss          ...
Masi, c             ...
Errickson, p        ...
Earley, p           ...
Totals             32  5 10 27 12

a-Batted for Wittig in 8th.
b-Batted for Carpenter in 8th.
c-Ran for Hale in 8th.
Giants           ...... 000 000 400—4
Braves           ...... 002 010 002x—5

Errors—None. Runs batted in—
Young, Jurges 3, Sisti, Cooney, West.
Two-base hits—Sisti, Cooney, West.
Young, Jurges, Sisti, Cooney, West.
Double plays—Hale, Jurges and O'Dea; Young, Carpenter, Jurges; Young.
Left on bases—Giants 6, Braves 7.
Bases on balls—off Wittig 1, Carpenter 1, Errickson 3, Earley 1.
Struck out—by Wittig 1, Carpenter 2-b, Errickson 2, Earley 3.
Hits—off Wittig, 5 in 4 innings;
Adams, 4 in 2, Carpenter 2 in 1,
Errickson, 4 in 2 1-3; Earley, 1 in 1 2-3. Runs—off Wittig 3, Errickson 1.
Wild pitch—Wittig. Winning pitcher—Earley.
```

HOME RUN BY JOE BLACKS OUT KEELER'S MARK

Red Sox Tried Hard to Stop Yankee Star; Dodgers Move Up

BY PAUL SCHEFFELS
(United Press Staff Correspondent)
New York, July 3 — (UP) — The hero of the hour, of course, is outfielder Joe DiMaggio of the New York Yankees who set a new major league batting record by hitting safely in his 45th consecutive game yesterday, but spare a thought for the deeds of another outfielder, Ted Williams of the Boston Red Sox.

DiMaggio today is the all-round batting star of the major leagues—that is, until you come to the batting averages and there, perched at the top, .053 percentage points ahead of "Pal Joey," is Williams with a league-leading mark of .407.

Comparatively little attention has been paid Williams' hitting achievements but if ever anybody is to crowd DiMaggio out of the American league batting picture, it will be this laconic, young left-handed slugger. The battle for the league batting title should be as interesting as the pennant fight.

Yanks Three Up

The Yankees defeated the Red Sox, 8-4 for their sixth straight win, ran their American league lead over the idle Cleveland Indians to three games and Williams added another hit to his already impressive average but the crowd of 8,682 had cheers only for DiMaggio.

Joe blasted a 400-foot homer into the left field stands, his 18th of the season, in the fifth inning off rookie Dick Newsome, 31-year-old right-hander. Joe's blow shoved Wee Willie Keeler's 44-year-old record into the obscurity baseball accords all "second-raters."

Newsome, with the aid of sparkling fielding by his teammates, had stopped DiMaggio in his first two trips. Stan Spence made a running, over-his-head catch of DiMaggio's hard liner in the first inning and third baseman Jim Tabor thrilled the crowd with a remarkable stop of a hot bounder in the third.

Then with the count two balls and one strike, DiMaggio slammed out the four-bagger that preserved the most sensational hitting streak in baseball.

Here's a comparison of Keeler's and DiMaggio's records:

```
         G AB R H 2b 3b HR TR Pct
DiMa'gio 45 179 67 12 3 13 124 .375
Keeler   44 201 82 11 10 0 113 .408
```

Buck Gets "Hot"

Buck Newsom, pride pitching flop of 1941, reverted to the form that brought him 21 victories in 1940, as the Detroit Tigers blanked the Chicago White Sox, 1-0 last night. Newsom, who had failed to go the route since June 11, allowed only three hits to break a three-game individual losing streak and won his sixth victory against 11 defeats. Pat Mullin's single, Charlie Gehringer's sacrifice and Rudy York's double scored the winning run. Mullin sustained a dislocated shoulder when he crashed into Sox pitcher Bill Dietrich in a play at first base.

Bob Johnson hit his 17th homer in the 10th inning to give the Philadelphia athletics a 7-6 triumph over the Washington Senators. It was the A's third straight win and their eighth in 12 starts.

Close to Top

The Brooklyn Dodgers climbed to within a half game of first place in the National league by knocking off the Philadelphia Phillies, 9-3 while the leading St. Louis Cardinals were idle. Kirby Higbe, Dodgers' "Iron Man" pitcher, appeared in his 23d game of the season—more than any other major league hurler—but allowed nine hits in 3 1-3 innings and was relieved by Bret Kimball, who pitched one-hit ball the rest of the way to get credit for the win.

The Pittsburgh Pirates whipped the Cincinnati Reds, 8-2. Max Butcher gave up 13 hits but staggered to his seventh win while Paul Derringer lost his 10th decision.

New York split with the Boston Braves. The Braves captured the opener, 5-4 but dropped the nightcap, 8-0 to Bill Lohrman's four-hitter.

YESTERDAY'S HERO — Joe DiMaggio of the New York Yankees who blasted his 18th homer of the year to set a new major league record for hitting safely in 45 consecutive games as his team defeated the Boston Red Sox, 8-4.

West Coast Pitcher Close To Gamblers

Durham, N. C., July 3—(UP)—Pitcher Julio Bonetti of Los Angeles in the Pacific Coast league, has been placed on baseball's ineligible list by President W. G. Bramham of the National Association of Minor Leagues. Bramham charged that Bonetti has associated with gamblers.

The decision followed a two-month investigation by Bramham, the district attorney's office of Los Angeles and a private investigator employed by the Los Angeles club. Bramham said Bonetti, who has been playing professional ball since 1933 and has had trials with the St. Louis Browns and Chicago Cubs, was seen talking money from a bookmaker on race horses and other sporting events.

PROBABLE PITCHERS

(By United Press)
National League
St. Louis (Lanier 8-3) at Chicago (Passeau 7-7).
Boston (Javery 8-1) vs.
Cincinnati (Pearson 1-2) at Pittsburgh (Lanning 3-4).
(Only games scheduled).

American League
Boston (Wagner 3-6) at Philadelphia (Dean 3-3).
(Only games scheduled).

Another For The Book

When Joe DiMaggio gets hot after records, there are no half-baked measures. He's pictured getting a great big hand from teammate Red Rolfe after crossing the plate with a homer during the Yankees-Red Sox game at New York. This Sullivan looks on. DiMag's four-bagger extended his batting streak to 45 consecutive games, blasting the all-time major league record set 44 years ago by Wee Willie Keeler.

Eyes Of All States Are On Illinois' Bookie-Bet Bill

BY JOE WILLIAMS

Chicago, July 3.—Changing trains on our way to Denver and the P. G. A. championship we found this mid-west metropolis cracking nervously on letter books and wondering out loud what the governor is going to do about that bill.

"That bill" is a legislative device which would legalize wide open betting on the horses in downtown stores, suburban pubs and even in the far flung hayseed districts of Illinois. The bill has passed both houses and is now on the governor's desk awaiting veto or signature. Opinion is confusedly divided as to what the governor's action will be. Some of the local sports writers we talked with are of the belief he will give it the green light. The top bookie in town, an acquaintance of many years, and a gentleman who usually knows all the answers, politically and otherwise, doesn't think it will be signed.

"The governor must think of the next election," pointed out Mr. Bookie, "and too many of the better people are opposed to the bill." Still, there was a possibility Mr. Bookie admitted, that the governor might diplomatically ignore the bill thus permitting it to become a law without his signature. "In that event he could at least say he didn't sign it," explained Mr. Bookie who knows all the amusing angles, too.

Good Governor Green

The governor in question is Dwight Green who is known as a clean government man. He's the gent who broke up the Capone mob (if indeed it is broken up) and helped put the fabulous Al behind the bars. His attorney general, one Courtney, is opposed to the bill and is known to be influential in the chief executive's official family. It was Courtney who led the Carrie Nation-like raids on Chicago and Cicero bookie some time back, demolishing the horse stores with axes and sledge hammers.

You still can bet with the bookies around here, but the play is nothing like it was in the days when practically every other entrance led to a pool room, many of them outfitted in the luxurious manner of private clubs, even including smart dining rooms, bars and faultless service. That phase of Chicago's horse betting is a joke forever. It started to go when the federal government closed in on old Moe Annenberg who carried over the racket not only here but all over America. Old Moe paid a stiff fine and went to jail and is still there. Today there isn't much left of the vast empire he built up and ruled over with a brutal, ruthless hand.

So many factors, principally an energetic federal drive, and operating against the pool room bookie that the racket is virtually in the death throes. Its only chance to come back in any fashion like the halcyon past know remote or favorable that chance is nobody can say for sure. If Governor Green should surprisingly break the ice over money-hungry states would follow suit. That has been the history of legalized betting at the tracks. One state followed another with identical bills. The selling point has always been these days. The state treasury is enriched, and supposedly this reduces taxes—and to a faint extent it does.

This isn't the first time a bookie-betting bill has come before an Illinois governor for his okay. Six years ago a similar bill was presented to the then Governor Horner, and he gave it the old heave-ho, adding that it was a "particularly vicious and unhealthy thing, unworthy of the serious consideration of any statesman who professed to have the best interest of the community at heart. This may have been a good break for clean government but it turned out to be an even better break for the bookie bookies. They were able to get the kind of protection they must always have to operate, and they proceeded to enjoy a string of lush, lucrative years.

Obviously the race track people out here are opposed to the bill, and it may be assumed they have been active—active in the way it counts most—in their opposition. It isn't difficult to understand this opposition. Only a small percentage of race goers patronize the tracks to see the horses run; their main interest is in making a bet. If they can walk into a convenient store and make a bet, certain of track odds and prompt pay offs, it seems reasonable to assume they aren't going to bother about going to the tracks. That a situation of this sort would cut deep into the tracks' financial resources, and in the end compel drastic curtailment in racing programs and purse distributions can scarcely be questioned.

Just the same we fear the legalized bookie is on his way, and the only thing that can stop him is an organized, intelligent propaganda drive, stressing the better things of racing, the breeding, the enormous investments and—the not unimportant outlet for employment. Even this may not be successful but it would be a deterrent. In any event, the forces for the legalized bookie are beginning to form. They are significant straws in the wind. And, to repeat, with the first break in the ranks—the first legalized action—there will be a stampede to get on the tax-reducing band wagon.

Baseball Standings

AMERICAN LEAGUE

Standings:
```
             W.  L.  Pct
New York     44  22  .667
Cleveland    41  25  .621
Boston       36  32  .529
Chicago      33  34  .493
Detroit      34  36  .486
Philadelphia 31  36  .463
Washington   29  37  .439
St. Louis    23  43  .348
```

Games Yesterday
New York 8, Boston 4.
Philadel. 7, Washington 6 (10 ins).
Detroit 1, Chicago 0 (night).
(Only games scheduled).

Games Today
Boston at Philadelphia.
(Only game scheduled).

Games Tomorrow
Washington at New York (2).
Boston at Philadelphia (2).
Chicago at Detroit (2).
St. Louis at Cleveland (2).

NATIONAL LEAGUE

Standings:
```
             W.  L.  Pct
St. Louis    45  22  .672
Brooklyn     44  23  .657
New York     36  29  .554
Cincinnati   31  30  .508
Chicago      31  35  .470
Pittsburgh   29  34  .460
Boston       28  38  .424
Philadelphia 15  48  .238
```

Games Yesterday
Brooklyn 9, Philadelphia 3.
Boston 5, New York 4 (1st).
New York 8, Boston 0 (2nd).
Pittsburgh 8, Cincinnati 2.
(Only games scheduled).

Games Today
St. Louis at Chicago.
Philadelphia at Boston (night).
(Only game scheduled).

Games Tomorrow
Philadelphia at Boston (2).
New York at Brooklyn (2).
St. Louis at Chicago (2).
Pittsburgh at Cincinnati (2).

EASTERN LEAGUE

Standings:
```
               W.  L.  Pct
Wilkes-Barre   40  27
Williamsport   39  28
Elmira         37  29
Scranton       35  32
Binghamton     31  34
Springfield    31  35
Hartford       26  39
Albany         25  40
```

Games Yesterday
Elmira 4, Hartford 3 (1st, night).
Elmira 4, Hartford 2 (2nd, night).
Springfield 6, Williamsport 4 (2nd, n).
Albany 6, Wilkes-Barre 3 (night).
Scranton 3, Binghamton 2 (1st, n).
Scranton 5, Binghamton 4 (2nd, n).

Games Today
Springfield at Hartford (8:30).
Wilkes-Barre at Albany.
Binghamton at Albany.
Homers by Dusak and Kobesky contributed to the downfall.

ONLY LOOKS LAME

Memory Book, veteran pointer, looks as if he is lame because out of a hind leg is shorter than the other

DAVIS NO MATCH FOR ZIVIC IN FISTIC "FLOP"

One-Sided Bout Ends in T. K. O. in Tenth; Less Than $37,000 Gate

BY JACK CUDDY
(United Press Staff Correspondent)
New York, July 3—(UP)—The real winner of last night's Zivic-Davis fiascaro were the thousands upon thousands of fans who has sense enough to stay away from the Polo Grounds.

For everyone else it was a double-barreled disappointment.

Promoter Mike Jacobs took a worse beating than Fritzie Bummy Davis, who suffered a technical knockout in the 10th round after blocking welterweight Champion Fritzie Zivic's left jab with a bloody schnozzola all evening.

Flopperoo

Summed up, this scheduled 12-round non-title bout was probably the most complete fiasco in the history of "big time" outdoor New York boxing.

The fight was a lop-sided dull, and the surprisingly small gathering of 8,986 fans contributed a gate of only $36,165 for the questionable privilege of witnessing it.

These figures proved a satisfactory punch to Promoter Jacobs' pocketbook. He had guaranteed the Army Relief society $10,000 of the gate in return for Private Davis' services. Or at least, that's what his publicity men stated. A 24-hour postponement and last night's threat of rain were factors in the debacle.

Hit the Deck

The opening round found moonfaced Bummy on the canvas for the first time in his career. A short straight right achieved the lone knockdown of the bout, and Bummy was just rising at the count of seven when the bell rang.

Thereafter Pittsburgh Fritzie contented himself with playing "Taps" on the artillery mess's bugle. No matter how or where Zivic thrust his left jab, Davis adroitly blocked it with his nose or mouth. No better catcher ever appeared there on the Giants' ball field.

After the fifth, it became apparent that it was merely a question of how long Davis could last—or how long referee Arthur Donovan would permit Zivic to continue sharpshooting at his bloody target. Came the eighth, and Bummy's nose looked like a squashed tomato and his lower lip seemed to have been slashed with a saber. Donovan wanted to stop the butchery at the end of the eighth, and again at the end of the ninth, but he listened to the pleas of Bummy's handlers.

He had to halt it at 2:12 of the 10th, after two body smashes almost jack-knifed Bummy, who was reeling around the ring holding his mid-section. It was Bummy's first kayo.

Zivic, who out-weighed Davis by the margin of 149½ pounds to 148, merely got a fair workout in preparation for his next two bouts. He meets Jimmy Barbera at Erie, Pa., on July 7 and on July 28 he defends his title against Red Cochrane of New Jersey at Ruppert's stadium in Newark.

Davis, on furlough from the army, returns to Uncle Sam on July 8.

How DiMaggio Set All-Time Mark

Game No. 45

FIRST INNING—Flied to Spence with the count one and one and was out on running catch, sharply to Tabor and was thrown out.

THIRD INNING—Grounded out.

FIFTH INNING—With count two and one, hit home run into left field stands.

SIXTH INNING—Hit first pitch and flied to Williams.

SEVENTH INNING—Hit a two and nothing pitch to Cronin, forcing Henrich at second.

Dial Doings
By JIM PARKER

The first lady of the theater, Helen Hayes, will make a Mutual network appearance tonight. She'll be heard over WATR at 8:15 in the weekly dramatization, "Sky Over Britain." Miss Hayes will take the leading role in "Two Fine the World Alone." Her part is that of Cornelia Baker, a British school teacher in a Midlands industrial town which is hit by an air raid. During the raid, which kills her father, she leads her class to an air raid shelter. The same raid orphans one of her students, a youngster brought to the nation will be heard on WATR tomorrow afternoon at 5 o'clock. The regular afternoon baseball game will be interrupted at that time for the Presidential broadcast . . . It has been rumored for some time that Guy Lombardo and his cosmetic sponsor were approaching the parting of the ways. Now comes word that Lombardo definitely is leaving the Monday night program and will be replaced by Freddy Martin's Orchestra.

WATR, your MBStation, tonight:
6:15, Scores with Bill Derwin;
6:30, Sports Page; 7, Fulton Lewis Jr.; 7:45, Orrin Tucker;
8, Wythe Williams; 8:45, Skinnay Ennis; 9:30, Dellenbrath; 10:30, The Great Gunns.

More shift from the microphone marts . . . Alice Frost asserts that in the legal world what is right and what is left is the clients. . . Phil Spitalny tells the one about the absent-minded cellist who rang up one of the waitresses and kissed his cash receipts good-bye . . . Charles (Johnny Presents) Martin claims that it's a rare man who can keep his head when a girl has taken everything else . . . Hi (Inner Sanctum) Brown says the only exercise some fellows get is chinning at the bar . . . Billy Mills says one way to get a man hot is to tell him he's done . . . Ezra Stone thinks Hitler is foolish to try and run a fence around the world because sooner or later he's bound to get the gate . . . Keenan Wynn says give a man a pony of brandy and he'll start to horse around . . . That's enough of that!

Busiest music man around radio these days is WOR's brilliant young composer-conductor-arranger Morton Gould . . . Currently, Gould is making original manuscript arrangements not only for his regular WATR-Mutual show, but for the pinch-hitting broadcasts he's doing for Major Bowes (the ailing Major selected Gould as his absinthe replacement). That adds up to an hour and a half of music a week to arrange, or a total of some 18 different arrangements. Each arrangement takes Gould from three to four hours. So now he's working from fourteen to eighteen hours a day, six days a week. He spends most of Sunday catching up on lost sleep.

Barry Wood has just been renewed for the eighth consecutive time on the Saturday night "Hit Parade". He's been on the show longer than any other male vocalist and is credited with having done much to keep the ratings of the broadcast at new high levels . . . Since Jose Iturbi was so disturbed over appearing on the same stage with Benny Goodman at the Robin Hood Dell Concert next week, he'll probably pass out completely when he realizes what confronts him on November 6. On that date Iturbi is supposed to conduct the orchestra in support of some harmonica-player Larry Adler, performing the first concerto ever written for mouth organ . . . Scheduled to conduct the Philadelphia Orchestra while Benny Goodman appears as soloist next Thursday night is Edwin McArthur. Although Jose Iturbi withdrew because he considered the assignment undignified, McArthur counts it as a "distinct honor and privilege" to appear with Goodman, "one of the towering personalities in modern music."

Because Bing Crosby and Don Ameche are afraid the boys in training camps are not getting in the folks back home enough about their daily work, the Thursday night show will undertake this task for the trainees . . . During the next few months, boys from various branches of the service will be guests on the show. The first of the series is Capt. Robert L. Denig, of the United States Marine Corps, who appears tonight. Capt. Denig has just completed a course in the operation of tanks. In past broadcasts, Crosby interviewed a man from a parachute battalion and a Naval flyer . . . In a talk with Ameche last week, Crosby said he had chatted with mothers who had sons in the various services and none of them seemed to know just what their sons were doing. Their letters usually mentioned food and recreation, but told little of the work to which the trainee was engaged. Mothers and friends of men in the services knew only the address and the fine of work. For example, one mother knew her son was in the cavalry, but she never knew about the cavalry other than the fact that cavalrymen rode horses.

New York Stations

WEAF—660 WOR—710 WJZ—770 WABC—880

All Listed Programs Are Daylight Saving Time

```
P. M.
4:00—WEAF—"Backstage Wife"
      WOR—Baseball Game;
      Cardinals vs. Cubs
      WJZ—"Mother o' Mine"
      WABC—Richard Maxwell
4:15—WEAF—"Stella Dallas,"
      Sketch
      WABC—Club Matinee,
      Variety
4:30—WEAF—"Lorenzo Jones"
      WJZ—"Young Widder
      Brown"
      WJZ—Allen Prescott, News
4:45—WEAF—"Home of the
      Brave"
      WOR—News, F. Singiser
      WABC—"Story of Mary
      Marlin"
5:00—WEAF—"Portia Faces
      Life"
      WJZ—"The Bartons,"
      Drama
      WABC—"We, the Abbotts"
5:15—WEAF—"Jack Armstrong"
      WOR—"Capt. Midnight"
      WJZ—Ray O'Neill,
      Drama
5:30—WEAF—"Three Runs,"
      Scores
      WOR—Uncle Don
      WJZ—News, Defense News
      WABC—Edwin C. Hill
5:45—WEAF—Don Goddard
      WOR—The World Today
      WJZ—Bill Stern, Sports
      WABC—"Scattergood
      Baines"
6:00—WEAF—News of the World
      WOR—News, F. Singiser
      WJZ—News, Alger's
      Orch.
      WABC—"Bobby Benson"
6:15—WEAF—Paul Sullivan,
      News
      WOR—"Hot Douglas,"
      Sport
      WJZ—News, H. R. Baukhage
      WABC—Fred Waring's
      Orch.
6:30—WEAF—Here's Morgan
      WOR—Sports, Stan Lomax
      WJZ—"Mary Ames," Sketch
      WABC—Paul Sullivan
6:45—WEAF—The World Today
      WOR—Fred Waring's Orch.
      WJZ—"Lowell Thomas"
      WABC—The World Today
7:00—WEAF—Fred Waring
      WOR—"Fulton Lewis Jr."
      WJZ—Easy Aces, Sketch
      WABC—Amos 'n' Andy
7:15—WEAF—"European News"
      WOR—"Lanny Ross," Tenor
      WJZ—Capt. Zumbro
      WABC—Lanny Ross, Songs
      WABC—"Confidentially Yours"
      News
7:30—WEAF—Horace Heidt's Orch.
      WOR—Gabriel Heatter,
      Commentator
      WJZ—"Pot o' Gold"
      WABC—"Mr. Keen, Tracer
      of Lost Persons"
7:45—WEAF—H. V. Kaltenborn,
      News
      WOR—"Inside of Sports"
      WABC—"Friends of Andy
      Kirk"
8:00—WEAF—"Maxwell Coffee
      Time"
      WOR—"Confidential"
      WJZ—"Earl Godwin," News
      WABC—"Death Valley Days"
8:15—WJZ—"Uncle Walter's
      Dog House"
      WABC—"Green Valley"
8:30—WEAF—"Aldrich Family"
      WOR—"Murder Clinic"
      WJZ—"News, John McCormick"
      WABC—"Public Affairs"
8:45—WABC—"Professor Quiz"
9:00—WEAF—"Good Neighbors,"
      Drama
      WOR—"Sinfonietta"
      WJZ—"America's Town
      Meeting"
      WABC—"Major Bowes'
      Amateur Hour"
9:30—WEAF—Bob Burns' Variety
      Show
      WJZ—"National Symphony
      Orch. Concert"
      WABC—"Glenn Miller's
      Orch."
10:00—WEAF—"Rudy Vallee's
      Variety Show"
      WOR—News, Berlin News
      WABC—"Professor Quiz"
10:15—WOR—Symphonic Strings;
      Strings
10:30—WEAF—"March of Time,"
      News
      WOR—Raymond Gram Swing,
      News
      WJZ—"News; Harry James'
      Band"
      WABC—"Juan Arvizu, Songs;
      Novak"
      WJZ—Ruth Lyon, Songs
11:00—News
```

```
1590—WBRY—96
P. M.
4:15—Columbia Concert Orch.
4:30—News, Musicale
4:45—Weather Forecast, News
4:50—Burl Ives, Baseball
5:00—News
6:00—Weather Forecast; News
6:05—"Your Marriage Club"
6:30—Elmer Davis and the News
6:45—The Shining Hour
7:00—U. S. Army Band
7:30—The Fred Piper, Jr.
      Presents
7:45—Edwin Miller Orch.,
      Presents
8:00—Allen Roth's Symphony of
      Melody
8:30—News
9:45—Musical Interlude...
9:00—Family, Ezra Stone
9:30—Colonel Stoopnagle
10:00—"Mr. Michael Loring's Orch.
10:45—Sign off.

1080—WTIC—288
P. M.
4:00—"Backstage Wife"
4:15—"Stella Dallas"
4:30—"Lorenzo Jones"
4:45—"Young Widder Brown"
5:00—"House of the Brave"
5:15—"Portia Faces Life"
5:30—"We, the Abbotts"
5:45—"Diane Courtenay,
      Sketch"
6:00—"Lorenzo Jones"
6:15—"House of the Brave"
6:30—"Portia Faces Life"
6:45—"Baseball Scores and
      Weather"
7:00—Musical Roundup
7:10—Stamp Collection
7:15—Frank Morgan
7:30—"Mystery at the Museum"
7:45—Baseball Scores
7:55—Post Newsman
8:00—"Professor Quiz"
8:15—Movie Tips
8:30—"Honeymoon Blues"
8:45—Jack Berch's Orch.
9:00—"Bob Hope's Pepsodent Show"
9:30—"Uncle Walter's Dog
      House"
10:00—"Rudy Vallee's Variety"
10:30—"March of Time"
11:00—News
11:15—Lloyd Hunts'
11:30—Harry James' Orch.,
      Entered
11:45—Charlie Spivak's Orch.
12:00—News
12:05—Van Alexander's Orch.
12:30—Robbins Orch.
1:00—Sign Off.

A. M.
TOMORROW
7:00—News
7:15—Weather Forecast
7:45—News, Musicale
8:15—Andy Jacobson's Rhythm
      Boys
8:30—Shopper's Guide
8:45—Front Page Farrell
9:00—Mrs. Wiggs of the Cabbage
      Patch
9:15—John's Other Wife
9:30—Just Plain Bill
9:45—Woman in White
10:00—David Harum
10:15—Against the Storm
10:30—Light of the World
10:45—Arnold Grimm's Daughter
11:00—The O'Neills
11:15—Guiding Light
11:30—Hymns of All Churches
11:45—News
```

```
WATR PROGRAMS
1320 Kilocycles
```

```
3:00—Braves vs. Phillies
5:30—News, Musicale
5:45—Melody News
6:00—To Be Announced
6:15—Dinner Music
6:30—News, Scores with Bill Derwin
6:45—Sports Page, Bill Barrows
7:00—Yankee News, Paul Young
7:15—Tomorrow's Headlines
7:30—Fulton Lewis Jr.
7:45—Musicale
8:00—Wythe Williams, Commentator
8:30—"Sky over Britain"
8:45—Skinnay Ennis' Orch.
9:00—To Be Announced
9:15—News; Jimmy Joy
9:30—Dellenbrath
10:00—"The Great Gunns"
10:30—Bill Leonard, Commentator
10:45—Nat Brandwynne's Orch.
11:00—News; Ted Lewis' Orch.
11:30—Mel Marvin's Orch.
11:55—News
12:00—Sign off.
```

```
LITTLE VARIANCE
Albany certified by the American
Bowling Congress cannot vary more
than a 32nd of an inch in width or
2-64ths in thickness.
```

and severe slump that dropped his average all the way to .363. Through it all, he never lost faith in his ability to hit. "Here's the way I look at it," he stated. "If I hit .400 this year everyone'll say I'm great. Then if I do slip to .200 next season, everyone will holler, 'He's just a flash in the pan.' But I'll tell you one thing. There'll always be one guy who believes William can hit—that's old Ted himself."

His belief paid off. As suddenly as he had gone into the slump, he came out of it. And with a vengeance. By the middle of June, he was back over .400. In early July, in a doubleheader on the last Sunday before the all-star game break, he belted out four hits in eight at bats and went into the all-star game hitting .405.

There has never been a greater or more dramatic Major League Baseball All-Star Game than the one that took place before 54,674 fans at Detroit's Briggs Stadium on July 8, 1941. In Europe that day, invading German troops pushed deeper into Russia, capturing Pskov, one of the Russian Empire's oldest cities. But Americans cast these worrying events aside to cheer on the most star-studded lineups of any previous all-star classic. The rosters of the two teams included eighteen future Hall of Famers, among

THE BASES WERE LOADED, THERE WAS ONLY ONE OUT, AND JOE DIMAGGIO AND TED WILLIAMS WERE COMING UP.

them pitching greats Bob Feller, Rod Ruffing, and Carl Hubbell, and hitting stars Lou Boudreau, Bobby Doerr, Mel Ott, and Johnny Mize. The two most closely watched players on the field—both on the American League side—were Joe DiMaggio, whose historic hitting streak was still alive at forty-seven games, and Ted Williams, hot in pursuit of the magic .400.

From the inaugural all-star game in 1933, the American League had ruled the classic, winning five of the first seven games played. But in 1940, the

National League notched their first victory, shutting out their rivals 4-0. That same year, a National League team won the World Series for the first time in six years. In 1941, the American League all-stars, led by DiMaggio and Williams, arrived in Detroit determined to exact revenge.

And after six innings, with the American Leaguers leading 2-1, they were on their way to getting it. But in the seventh, a two-run homer from the Dodgers' Arky Vaughan put the Nationals ahead 3-2. Then, in the top of the eighth, another two-run homer from Vaughan extended the National League's lead to 5-2. A National League victory—with Vaughan the undisputed hero of the game—seemed assured.

At least until, in the bottom of the eighth, Joe DiMaggio and his brother Dominic of the Red Sox both stroked doubles, cutting the Nationals' lead to 5-3. In the bottom of the ninth, the American League came to bat for the final time, hoping to close the two-run deficit. The Cubs' outstanding right-hander Claude Passeau was on the mound, and he got the first batter to pop up to the second baseman, putting the National League just two outs away from victory. The Indians' Ken Keltner was next up. He hit a ground ball directly at the shortstop that seemed to be a sure second out, but it took a bad hop, striking the infielder on his shoulder and leaving Keltner safe at first. The next batter, the Yankees' Joe Gordon, singled sharply to right. When Passeau walked the next hitter on a 3-2 count, the predominantly American League crowd went wild. And with good reason. The bases were loaded, there was only one out, and Joe DiMaggio and Ted Williams were coming up.

Williams and Joe DiMaggio became enthusiastic, open admirers of each other's baseball abilities.

Williams crosses the plate after hitting one of the most famous home runs in baseball history—his two-out, ninth-inning game-winning home run in the 1941 All-Star Game.

The great DiMaggio stepped to the plate. With the crowd pleading for the man who was in the midst of an incredible forty-seven-game hitting streak to get one more *right now*, the Yankee slugger hit a ground ball straight to the shortstop. It should've been a game-ending double play, but the shortstop's throw to the second baseman was a little off line, which meant the relay throw to first pulled the first baseman off the bag. DiMaggio was safe, and the American League was still alive.

With the score now 5-4, two outs, and the tying run on third and the winning run on first, Ted Williams came to the plate. "Passeau was always tough," Williams would later write. "He had a fast tailing ball he'd jam a left-hand hitter with, right into your fists, and if you weren't quick he'd get it past you." But Williams had studied Passeau more carefully than anybody, and he was ready. "He worked the count to two balls and one strike, then he came in with that sliding fastball around my belt, and I swung."

And as he had been doing all season long, Williams connected. "I had pulled it to right field, no doubt about that," he eventually remembered. "But I was afraid that I hadn't got enough of the bat on the ball. But gee, it just kept going up, up, way up into the right-field stands."

The game was over. The American League had won 7-5. As Williams rounded the bases, "clapping his hands and leaping like a young colt," the entire American League waited for him at home plate, ready to carry him off the field in triumph. He would win six batting titles, hit 450 more home runs, and be elected to the Hall of Fame. But for the rest of his life, Ted Williams would proclaim that his 1941 all-star game home run was "the most thrilling hit of my life."

Ecstatic as Williams was about his performance, he had little time to revel in it. He was pursuing a bigger goal. And buoyed by his all-star heroics, he remained hot with the bat throughout the rest of July. Despite a few hitless days in August, he was able to stay comfortably above .400 and entered the second week of September hitting a hefty .412. At this point, his quest for .400 was gripping the nation about as strongly as DiMaggio's hitting streak had a few months earlier. The pages of the newspapers were filled with reports from the war zones but from coast-to-coast had a daily feature detailing what Williams had done the previous day, what he was now hitting, and what he had to do until the end of the season to finish at .400. Radio stations everywhere ended their newscasts with reports on the Splendid Splinter's batting average. In one of the most interesting developments, Williams's teammates, who had long regarded him as a spoiled superstar, began openly rooting for him every time he came to bat.

It all took its toll. Feeling more pressure than he had ever experienced

American League All-Star manager Del Baker demonstrates his appreciation for Williams's All-Star game dramatics.

The higher his batting average rose, the more national and even worldwide attention Williams attracted. Here he demonstrates his batting stance for movie cameramen.

GREAT ALL-STAR GAME MOMENTS

Ted Williams's dramatic ninth-inning game-winning home run was unquestionably the greatest single moment in all-star game history, but over the years the star-studded game has provided other great thrills as well.

1933   Babe Ruth hits the first home run in all-star game history. The first all-star game was supposed to be a one-time affair, but Ruth's towering home run galvanized such enthusiasm for the game that it became a fixture on the baseball calendar.

1934   The American League was represented by a remarkably powerful lineup. But in what remains one of the greatest pitching feats ever, the National League's Carl Hubbell struck out five future Hall of Famers in a row—Babe Ruth, Lou Gehrig, Jimmie Foxx, Al Simmons, and Joe Cronin.

1949   Even though Jackie Robinson broke the color barrier in 1947, it took two more years before African American ballplayers were selected for the all-star game. The 1949 game made history when the Dodgers' Robinson, Roy Campanella, and Don Newcombe, and the Indians' Larry Doby took the field.

1955   At the end of the sixth inning, the National League trailed the American League 5-0. But in the seventh, the Nationals scored two runs, followed by three more in the eighth to tie the score. The game remained deadlocked until the bottom of the twelfth when

Stan Musial, appearing in his tenth straight all-star game for the National League, drilled a game-winning walk-off home run.

1971 In the bottom of the third inning of the all-star game held in Detroit's Tiger Stadium, Reggie Jackson was sent up to pinch-hit for his Oakland A's teammate, pitcher Vida Blue. Jackson blasted the ball an amazing 520 feet before it smashed into a transformer attached to one of the light towers on the stadium's roof. It remains the longest home run in all-star game history.

1999 The Boston Red Sox's Pedro Martinez was arguably the best pitcher in baseball when he started for the American League in the 1999 all-star game held in Boston's Fenway Park. In the first inning, Martinez struck out Barry Larkin, Larry Walker, and Sammy Sosa. In the second, he struck out Mark McGwire. Then, after the next batter reached on an error, he struck out Jeff Bagwell. Five strikeouts of all-star players in two innings. Not in succession (as Carl Hubbell had done in 1934) but spectacular enough to make Martinez the game's most valuable player and the first American League pitcher to win the all-star game in his home park.

2007 With a teammate on first base in a scoreless 2007 all-star game, American League power hitter Ichiro Suzuki drove a ball onto the deepest part of San Francisco's AT&T Park. As National League outfielder Ken Griffey ran frantically after the ball, it hit an all-star game banner and bounced wildly away from him. By the time he was able to retrieve the ball and throw it home, Ichiro had rounded the bases for the first and only inside-the-park home run in all-star game history.

in his baseball life, Williams went into his most serious slump of the season. From September 10 until September 21, he batted a measly .270. With just six games left in the season (three in Washington and three in Philadelphia), his average had fallen to .405, precisely where it had been during the all-star game break. At this point, in order to be as precise as possible, sportswriters were reporting his batting average in four decimal points (.4055, for example, rather than .406).

In the opening game against the Senators, Williams banged out one hit, just enough to keep his average at .405 (or more precisely .4051, compared to the .4055 it stood at entering the game). In the next day's doubleheader, he slipped badly, going one for seven and dropping his average to .401. Then it was off to Philadelphia for the final three games of the season—a single game on Saturday and a doubleheader on Sunday. Thanks to the newspapers and the radio, almost every baseball fan in America knew that two more outs would drop Williams's average below .400.

And that's just what happened in the opening game of the Athletics' series. The A's pitchers held him to one for four, putting his average at .399555. According to baseball tradition, that figure would be rounded off to an even .400, and that's how it would be listed in the record books. As early as the beginning of the Washington series when Williams's average was comfortably above .400, many folks had urged Red Sox manager Joe Cronin to keep Ted on the bench during the final Sunday doubleheader to preserve the coveted .400 mark. But was it *really* .400, or was it only .399555? Many of the nation's top newspapers made it clear how they felt. "STAR BATTER SLIPS BELOW .400" started the headline in *The New York Times*. "WILLIAMS DROPS BELOW .400 AS RED SOX DEFEAT A's" screamed *The*

Baseball experts, seeking to explain Williams's exceptional hitting powers, credited his amazing eyesight as the secret weapon of his success.

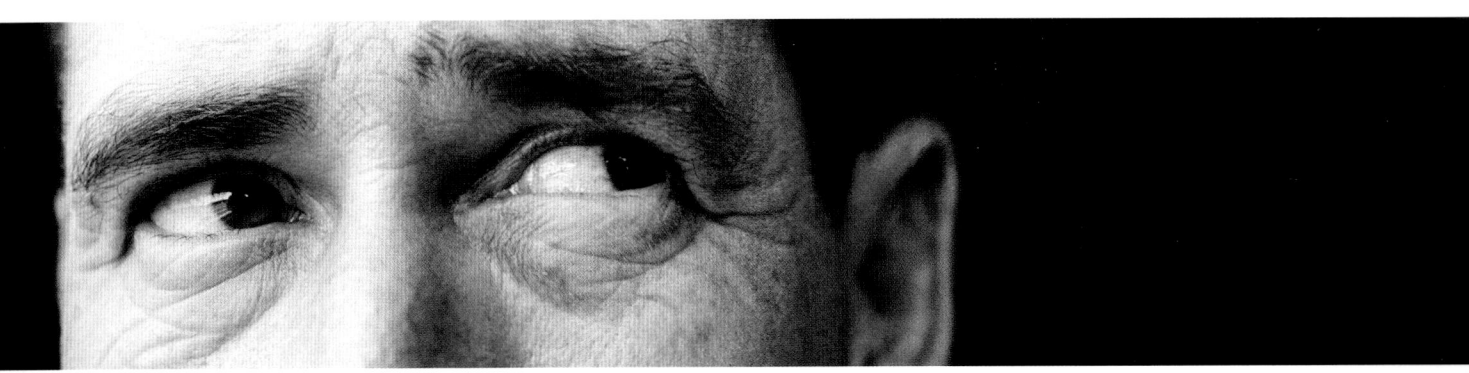

Washington Post. "SOX TOP A's WILLIAMS FALLS TO .399" read the headline in *The Philadelphia Inquirer*.

Despite the headlines, Cronin was seriously considering keeping Williams out of the lineup. As far as he was concerned, the rounded-off figure was legitimate: Williams had hit .400 and he deserved it. But Ted was having none of it. "If I'm going to be a .400 hitter," he declared, "I want more than my toenails on the line. If I can't hit .400 all the way, I don't deserve it."

Not that he wasn't worried about his great dream slipping away on the very last day of the season. He was particularly concerned about the doubleheader being played on the Athletics' home field. "Shibe Park," stated Joe Cronin, "is the roughest ballpark in the world to hit in this time of year. The afternoon shadows from those high stands make it awfully tough on a batter in September. The pitcher is in the sun and the plate is in the shadows, and you can't see the ball. And Daylight Savings ends on Sunday. It could be pretty dark by the time the second game gets underway."

> "THE PITCHER IS IN THE SUN AND THE PLATE IS IN THE SHADOWS, AND YOU CAN'T SEE THE BALL."

Williams had another concern as well. No hitter in baseball spent more time studying pitchers than did Ted. No hitter knew better than he what a certain pitcher was likely to throw at him in a specific situation. But here at the very end of the season, he was likely to be batting against young pitchers he had never faced before who had been brought up to the big leagues as a reward for having had a good minor league season.

The night before the final two games, Williams was simply too keyed up to sleep. He recruited his friend, Red Sox equipment manager Johnny Orlando, to join him on a three-hour-plus walk through the darkened city. "I walked all over Philadelphia," Williams remembered, "talking about what I had to do, worried about whether I could do it . . . and talking about the pitchers I was going to have to face the next day." The pressure was on, and Williams was laser focused. "I kept thinking about the thousands of swings I had taken to prepare myself," he recounted long after his playing days were over. "I had practiced and practiced. I kept saying to myself 'you are ready.' I went to the ballpark the next day more eager to hit than I had ever been."

He was ready, but so too were the Athletics. As he stepped into the batter's box in the second inning of the first game to face Dick Fowler, a six-foot-four-and-one-half-inch rookie right-hander, the A's catcher, gave him a word: his manager Connie Mack "told us if we let up on you, he'll run us out of baseball. I wish you all the luck in the world, but we're not giving you a damn thing." More determined than ever, Williams dug in and, with the count 2-0, hit what the reporter for *The Boston Globe* described as "a sizzling single past first baseman Bob [Johnson]."

> In major league ballparks, if a batted ball lands in fair territory and then bounces into the stands, it's declared a "ground rule double" and the player who hit it is granted second base.

With his average now .40089, he came up against Fowler again in the fifth.

The experts had already calculated that if he made an out this time, he'd be hitting exactly .400. But he did not make an out. Instead, he drove a Fowler fastball more than 440 feet over the right-center field wall. It was his thirty-seventh round-tripper of the season, and he now led both leagues in home runs. More important, he was now batting .40222.

At this point, the game turned into a slug fest and Williams came up an inning later, this time against left-hander Porter Vaughan. With the count 2-0, he grounded a hard single into right field. In the most pressure-packed game of his life, he was three for three; his average had risen to .404, and, as the game's announcers were informing everyone, he'd have to go hitless in his next five plate appearances to dip below .400.

Ted closed out the game with another single to right and a ninth-inning

When he passed away, the Red Sox decorated Fenway Park's left-field wall with a tribute to the legendary star.

grounder that was bobbled by the second baseman for a clean error. Williams had gone four for five. As he sat in the locker room between games, he was told that he could go zero for four in the second game and still wind up at .40044.

He had no intention of going zero for anything. His first time up, facing another rookie, Fred Caligiuri, he hit another ground ball single into right. At last, Ted Williams's great achievement was firmly in his grasp. But this was the "Splendid Splinter," "the Kid," "Teddy Ballgame," and he had one more gigantic thrill to provide. Batting against Caligiuri again in the fourth, he hit what one journalist described as the hardest clout that he had hit in his three seasons with the Red Sox. No one knows just how far the ball might have traveled had it not struck a speaker horn 460 feet from home plate. After shattering the horn, the ball dropped back on the field for what had to be one of the hardest-hit ground rule doubles in baseball history.

Williams's plaque at the Baseball Hall of Fame encapsulates a career that reads more like fiction than fact.

As the crowd and the Red Sox dugout and bullpen screamed in delight, Ted Williams stood on second, the seventh straight time he had been on base in the doubleheader.

He came up to bat one more time and, with darkness rapidly settling in, flied out to left field. On the most important day in his baseball career, he had gone six for eight. He had ended one of the most extraordinary individual baseball seasons in history with an official batting average of .40570,

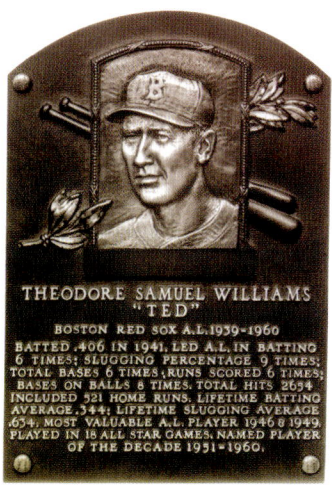

THE KID ♦ 59

Ted Williams was the epitome of the baseball star turned military hero. He left the game not once but twice to serve his country, first in World War II and then in the Korean War.

or, when rounded off, .406. "Can you imagine that kid," exclaimed manager Joe Cronin immediately after the game. "Four singles, a double and a homer when the chips were down. I tell you, I never came closer to bawling right out loud on a baseball diamond [than] when Ted got that third hit. I really filled right up. I was so happy that the kid had done the trick without asking or being given any favors."

Williams was too drained to say very much. But what he did say told it all. "What a thrill!" he said. "I wasn't saying much about it before the game, but I never wanted anything harder in my life."

For Ted Williams, there was more to this historic season than batting average alone. He had also led the major leagues in walks (147), on-base percentage (.553), slugging (.735), runs scored (135), and home runs (37). Perhaps most amazing of all, he had struck out only twenty-seven times. It was, declared *The New York Times*, "a 20th-century baseball masterpiece unlike any other, carved not across one World Series, one month, or even 56 games, but from April 15 to Sept. 18. Every single at-bat figured in the outcome."

In 1991, on the fiftieth anniversary of his hitting over .400, Williams reflected on his achievement. "It was something," he explained, "that required a kind of nonstop consistency. I never thought of it as going 2 for 5 every day, but that's what it adds up to. I had to maintain my focus throughout. Although I never imagined that all these years later, no one else would do it again."

One of the greatest tributes to Williams's 1941 season came from Harvard paleontologist and writer Stephen Jay Gould who called it "the greatest achievement in 20th-century hitting and a lesson to all who value the best in human possibility." Joe Cronin summed it up more simply. "Nobody," he stated, "could get him out."

WILL ANYONE EVER HIT .400 AGAIN?

It has been more than eighty years since Ted Williams hit .406 for the 1941 season. And one of the most common baseball questions continues to be, will anyone ever hit .400 again? Most baseball experts and former stars of the game consider the feat nearly impossible today.

"It will be difficult to maintain a .400 average over a full season," says former Kansas City Royals superstar George Brett, "because bullpens have become so important and so dominant. Starters usually go only five or six innings, then you have a reliever set up for the seventh, eighth and ninth innings, and they all have great stuff." Hall of Famer Rod Carew agrees. "You might see four or five pitchers during the game," he says, "younger guys who are fresh and throwing hard."

Former player and Hall of Fame manager Al Lopez cites another reason why, he believes, hitting .400 has become an impossible task: the fact that in Ted Williams's era, teams played most, if not all of their games, in the daytime. "Night baseball," states Lopez, "gives the pitcher an advantage he didn't have years ago. I know in my time a pitcher couldn't afford to rear back and fire for nine innings. We played all day baseball, and during that hot weather in July and August, a pitcher had to pace himself."

And finally, there is this from sports journalist Robert Kuenster. "Perhaps the biggest reason . . . that .400 hitters are considered museum pieces," he has written, "is the fact that most major leaguers today are aiming for the fences. Hitters strike out more because they are going for distance."

SEPIA BALL

AT THE MIDWAY POINT in the 1941 season, Ted Williams expressed his ambitions in an interview with the press. "I admit it," he said, "I love to hit. One of these years I aim to finish over .400. After all, I'm only twenty-three now and I ought to have a lot of chances before I'm done. I'm looking forward to the All-Star Game. Only the best of the best are allowed to play in it."

Actually, Williams was wrong. What he should have said was that only the best of the best *white* players were chosen to play in the all-star game. In 1941, Black players were not permitted in the major leagues. America's national pastime looked like the nation itself, where Black citizens were denied full rights and freedoms in countless ways, large and small.

America had two parallel societies and economies in 1941. Black dentists, doctors, lawyers, auto mechanics, professionals, and entrepreneurs of all sorts serviced the Black communities of cities and towns across the nation. A thriving Black press reported on relevant news. The military draft conscripting hundreds of thousands of young men into military service was enlisting them into completely separate service units, all white and all Black. And when people sought escape from

Like so many crowd-pleasing antics, umpiring in the Negro Leagues was often an attention-getter all its own.

HISTORY OF THE NEGRO LEAGUES

SINCE THE 1880S, Major League Baseball had effectively barred Black players. In 1920, a group of Black businesspeople led by the great Rube Foster had formed the Negro National League (NNL). The new league professionalized some of the independent "barnstorming" ball clubs that had been entertaining fans for decades prior.

Before the Negro Leagues were formed, teams of color supported themselves by barnstorming throughout the country. Early on, some of these teams had one or two white players.

For ten years, Foster's NNL showcased the dazzling talent of Black players. But then the Great Depression took its toll on baseball, and especially on Black baseball. Unemployment soared to 25 percent, and then as now, it was higher for Black people—close to double the jobless rate for white people. Attendance at white major league games dropped 20 percent, and in 1931, the NNL folded, its fans unable to afford even small diversions.

But Effa Manley—who would go on to become the only woman in the baseball Hall of Fame—and her husband Abe Manley, who co-owned the Newark Eagles, could not accept the absence of a proper league. In 1933, the Manleys and other Black club owners reconstituted the NNL. By 1941, economic conditions had improved enough nationally to support two Negro major leagues, the NNL and the Negro American League.

Both as a pitcher and a league executive, Rube Foster is widely viewed as the most important individual in Negro League history.

the dread of the coming combat, they watched baseball teams that were just as segregated.

And so, the 1941 baseball season was actually two seasons—one Black, one white. White baseball's "color line"—an unwritten agreement among white club owners and big-league management not to employ Black players, no matter how tremendous their talent—had been firmly in place since 1887. Black players were relegated to what are commonly called the Negro Leagues: an ever-shifting collection of semipro local ball clubs, paired with the top-level Negro National and Negro American Leagues. But "Negro Leagues" is a phrase seldom seen in the Black newspapers of 1941. In the Black press, the game was more commonly known as "sepia ball."

> **"ONLY ONE THING IS KEEPING THEM OUT OF THE BIG LEAGUES— THE COLOR OF THEIR SKIN..."**

In many ways, 1941 was poised to be a banner year for the Negro Leagues. Attendance and revenue had been steadily improving as the Depression receded, and the leagues' rosters were stacked with talent. The coming war would provide a boost to the leagues because it put more money in Black fans' pockets.

However, in many ways, 1941 also marked the beginning of the end for these star-studded all-Black leagues. In all areas of life, the approaching war was a catalyst for piercing questions about how America could fight for equality abroad without guaranteeing the same to its citizens at home. Black baseball players—and Black journalists, team managers, and fans alike—brought such questions to the ballfield.

For much of the twentieth century, Black-owned and staffed newspapers across the country covered communities and events that went almost completely ignored by the mainstream press. They celebrated Black achievement and chronicled injustice and anti-Black violence. Their opinion columns were replete with brilliantly crafted arguments for a better America.

The sports pages were no exception. Sportswriters on Black papers, such as Sam Lacy of the *Chicago Defender*, Ed Harris of *The Philadelphia Tribune*, Joe Bostic of New York's *The People's Voice*, and Dan Burley of the *New York Amsterdam Star-News*, all used their columns to advocate for the integration of the major leagues.

Black sportswriter Wendell Smith of the *Pittsburgh Courier* was one of the most vocal challengers of baseball's apartheid.

"In these days of world unrest, while our great President is standing on high and crying of the inhuman practices being carried on in other countries and shouting his political lungs out about freedom and democratic ideals, we feel that this is the time for Negroes the nation over to organize and fight for the Negro ball player," wrote Smith in 1939, the year German dictator Adolf Hitler launched World War II. "If we must, we should show Hitler and the rest of the world that compared with Uncle Sam he's not really so bad after all. The only difference is that his methods are a bit cruder."

And, the calls for change weren't just coming from Black voices—although white reporters often focused less on equality and more on how Major League Baseball could profit from these talented athletes. "There's a couple of million dollars worth of baseball talent on the loose ready for the big leagues, yet unsigned by any major leagues," wrote white columnist Shirley Povich of *The Washington Post* in March 1939. "Only one thing is keeping them out of the big leagues—the color of their skin . . ."

Almost from the time the first Negro Leagues were formed, protests were held urging the admission of Black players into the major leagues.

INCREDIBLE CHALLENGES

NEGRO LEAGUE PLAYERS played in a nation that professed to love freedom but practiced oppression in its day-to-day reality. That oppression meant Black players with first-rate ability were subjected to second-class conditions, on and off the baseball diamond. Their games were sometimes played in traditional stadiums, but at other times all they had access to were farmers' fields or scruffy vacant lots.

"Back in those days, we rode all night in the buses," recalled Ted "Double Duty" Radcliffe, who earned his nickname pitching the first game of a doubleheader and catching the second. "Sometimes we'd play four games a day."

Radcliffe also recalled what the South was like in his heyday during the Depression years. No public bathrooms for Black people. No restaurants. No hotels. These establishments existed, but they were all off-limits to people of color. The dividing line was enforced by state laws and the courts, and the ever-present threat of violence.

With the low pay—Radcliffe made one hundred dollars a month—Black players would often play twelve months a year just to make a living. They'd play in the United States February through October, then head for the Winter Leagues in Central America and Mexico. "We didn't go on a disabled list unless we were broken and in a wheelchair and on two crutches," Riley Stewart recalled. "If we got hurt, we played. We didn't have no relief pitcher. You go out there, you go for nine. That's it. You were paid for nine and that's the way they wanted you to pitch."

"We were worked like the mule that plows the fields all week and drives the carriage to church on Sunday," was how the always eloquent Satchel Paige put it. Yet despite all these hardships and more, the men who filled the

"Double Duty" Radcliffe attempts to tag out Homestead Grays superstar Josh Gibson.

ranks of the Negro Leagues loved what they had been given the opportunity to do.

"There were a lot of Black guys in the cotton patches in the South and other places that could play just as good as we could play," said Monte Irvin. "It was just the lucky ones that was given the chance."

"Their talents are being wasted in the rickety parks in the Negro sections of Pittsburgh, Philadelphia, New York, [and] Chicago," Povich continued. "It's a tight little boycott that the majors have set up against colored players."

Meanwhile, labor unions and civil rights groups picketed outside the major league parks of New York and Chicago to protest the sport's segregation. In 1940, at the New York World's Fair, the Trade Union Athletic Association staged an "End Jim Crow in Baseball" rally.

A few influential leaders in the white majors began to make their perspectives known—often prompted by the efforts of Black sportswriters. Leo Durocher, manager of the Brooklyn Dodgers, told the *Daily Worker* in 1939, "if the bosses said it was all right" he would hire Black players. In 1940, Gabby Hartnett of the Cubs echoed the sentiment to *Friday* magazine. "I am not interested in the color of a player, just his ability. If managers were given permission, there'd be a mad rush to sign up Negroes," Hartnett said.

Around this same time, Monte Irvin came close to becoming the first Black player to enter the major leagues, nine years before Jackie Robinson famously broke baseball's color barrier.

In high school in New Jersey, Irvin had been an all-star in four different sports. His astonishing talent prompted one of his teachers to write to the owner of the New York Giants, Horace Stoneham, informing him, "We have a player here you have to see to believe."

Stoneham sent a scout to watch Irvin play. Before the game was even over, he sent a report to the owner stating, "Could be the next Joe DiMaggio. Could be one of the greatest players I've ever seen."

Many baseball historians believe that if it hadn't been Jackie Robinson, the immensely talented Monte Irvin would have been first to break the color barrier.

It would take nine more years before Jackie Robinson was permitted to break the color barrier. It would be eleven more years after the scout's report that future Hall of Famer Irvin would be brought up to the Giants.

Eight years into Irvin's brilliant major league career, Horace Stoneham told him the story of the long-ago scout and his fantastic report. "What did you tell the scout?" Irvin asked.

"I said it was too soon," Stoneham replied. "I wish I'd been braver than that."

And so, in 1941, baseball's color line persisted—while most of the white press, and the white public, looked the other way, or even applauded the segregation.

Change *was* coming, and the war would propel it. But in 1941, most people had no idea that the beginning of the end for segregated baseball, and eventually for the Negro Leagues, was around the corner. With their loyal fans watching and the majors beginning to pay attention, too, Black baseball was prepared to put on the best show it could muster: the East-West All-Star Game. Created in 1933 by Negro National League founder Gus Greenlee, and usually held in Chicago's Comiskey Park, it was Black baseball's biggest draw. It was Black baseball's greatest spectacle. In fact, it was the number one event on the Black sports calendar.

Sam Lacy, the great sports journalist for *The Washington Tribune* and later the *Defender*, remembered the many East-West classics he covered for his newspapers. "It was a holiday for at least 48 hours," he wrote. "People would just come from everywhere, mainly because it was such a spectacle . . . I would go on my vacation during All-Star week so that I could be there the entire week. I didn't want to miss anything."

By 1941, the game had become an even greater event than its earliest supporters could have imagined. "The ninth annual East versus West baseball classic," the *Chicago Defender* told its readers, "will be played at Comiskey Park on Sunday afternoon July 27. The largest crowd in the history of the classic is expected out to watch the 1941 dream game. From the increased interest in the game each year, the 1939 record of 40,000 will be smashed."

It was actually an underestimation. Though it was played in ninety-seven-degree heat ("The bean was beamin' and I was steamin'," wrote the slightly balding Dan Burley, sports editor of the *New York Amsterdam*

Star-News), it drew 50,000 people, the largest crowd ever to attend a Black sporting event. And even though officials tried to cram every person into the ballpark, another 10,000 fans had to be turned away. "So many persons were refused admittance that 'a roving reporter' could make a delightful news story for the society pages about all of the splendid, if somewhat wilted costumes, and disappointed looking faces on the outside," wrote Elizabeth Galbreath, society reporter for the *Defender*.

"Fans came by auto, special train, excursions and street car from such states in the South as Louisiana, Mississippi, Texas, Alabama, Tennessee, Arkansas, Missouri, and Oklahoma. They came in droves from points in Ohio, Indiana, Michigan and as far west as Iowa to be part of this, the greatest gathering of Negroes at a sporting event in history. Only 2 percent of the crowd was white," reported the *Amsterdam Star-News*.

So, this game—the last peacetime East-West game before the breaking of the color barrier—was the most remarkable moment of the '41 season for Black baseball, a small but noticeable milestone in the long path forward for civil rights. Black fans were eager to see the stars, and rightly so given their immense

Effa Manley is the first and only woman with a plaque in the National Baseball Hall of Fame. The longtime owner of the Newark Eagles of the Negro National League, Manley was inducted into the Hall in 2006.

Comiskey Park was the site of the 1941 East vs. West Game and of other Negro League baseball contests.

The annual East vs. West All-Star classic was for years the most anticipated, publicized, and well-attended game in Sepia Ball.

talent. But the game was about more than that. The event strengthened a sense of pride in community for Black people. And the athletes put the lie to the ongoing, nonsensical insistence of many baseball executives that "colored" players weren't the equal of their white counterparts.

"Let me tell you a little bit about the East-West game," Negro Leagues great Buck O'Neill wrote in his autobiography. "Because for a Black ballplayer and Black baseball fans, that was something special . . . It made Black people feel involved in baseball like they'd never been before. While the big leagues left the choice of players up to the sports writers, [the Negro Leagues] left it up to the fans.

"After reading about the great players in the *Chicago Defender* and *The Pittsburgh Courier* for so many years, they could cut out the ballot in [these] Black papers, send it in and have a say. This was a pretty important thing for Black people to do in those days, to be able to vote, even if it was just for ballplayers, and they sent in thousands and thousands of ballots. It was like an avalanche."

More than 275,000 fans sent in their votes for the 1941 East-West game. And through voting, they compiled two powerhouse rosters.

The East team was anchored by first baseman Buck Leonard, who's been called the "Black Lou Gehrig"—though some have called Lou Gehrig the "White Buck Leonard." Leonard was at the height of his career as one of the top ten players in Negro League history, and one of the top hundred players of all time, period. League statistics, imperfect though they are, have Leonard batting .345 for his career with a .589 slugging percentage over 2,541 plate appearances.

Leonard spent all fifteen years of his career with the mighty Homestead Grays of the Negro American League—no other player played as many seasons for a single Black major league team—and he was central to their might.

"Buck Leonard was as smooth a first baseman as I ever saw," said Grays booking agent Eddie Gottlieb. "In those days, the first baseman on a team in the Negro Leagues often played the clown. They had a funny way of catching the ball so the fans would laugh, but Leonard was strictly baseball—a great glove, a [heck] of a hitter, and drove in runs."

Monte Irvin, who played with Leonard in the '41 game, said of him, "Trying to sneak a fastball by him was like trying to sneak a sunrise past a rooster." It was certainly true in 1941, when he led the league in home runs—and in seven other offensive categories.

Buck Leonard, shown here beating out an infield hit, was one of the most accomplished players and one of the most articulate spokesmen for Negro League ball players.

Roy Campanella was among the first Negro League players to be finally allowed into the major leagues. Both as a catcher and a hitter, he was an All-Star in every sense of the word.

Universally described as a gentleman, a natural leader with his quiet dignity, poise, and agreeable personality, Leonard was more essential to his ball club than ever before in 1941. His longtime teammate Josh Gibson, now recognized as baseball's all-time batting average leader, had jumped to the Mexican League in 1940.

Another star on the 1941 Eastern all-star team was catcher Roy Campanella.

Campanella had been recruited by the Washington (later Baltimore) Elite Giants at age fifteen—becoming perhaps the youngest player in Negro Leagues history. He started as the third-string catcher, but quickly got the starting job. By 1941, just twenty, Campanella was so well known by Black

78 ♦ BASEBALL'S SHINING SEASON

fans that in the summer he received more than 187,000 votes for his first all-star game.

By the summer of '41, Campanella had already been drafted by the military—in April, actually. "The United States wasn't at war yet, but the boys were being called up from everywhere," he wrote in his autobiography. "If Uncle Sam wanted me, I was ready, for whatever job he had in mind for me."

That turned out to be a job in a defense plant, and it looked like he might not be able to join the Elite Giants. But he worked out a way to keep playing ball while staying in touch with the plant if he was needed, and managed to play the whole season.

Unlike some of the truly tragic figures around Black baseball in the 1940s—men like Buck Leonard who just missed out on gaining full recognition and respect for their greatness during their playing days—Campanella was young enough that he was able to rise to glory as a full major leaguer. He won a World Series with the Dodgers in 1955 and was MVP of the National League three times in the 1950s.

Facing off against Campy, Leonard, and all the rest of the Eastern all-stars was an equally formidable lineup from the West, anchored by two generationally talented pitchers.

The top vote getter of the event was no surprise—Satchel Paige, the face of Black baseball for twenty years, its greatest talent and greatest attraction. If the 1941 East-West game stood out for anything, it was the size of the crowd—and the crowd was lured to the ballpark above all by the knowledge they'd see "Satch."

This six-feet, three-inches, 130-pound pitcher got his nickname when, as a young man, he helped support his large, impoverished family by carrying suitcases at a train station. Leroy Robert "Satchel" Paige was not only the best pitcher in Black baseball; he was also, in the opinion of many, the best pitcher of all time. Joe DiMaggio was quoted as saying, "I can't hit Satchel Paige. The best and fastest pitcher I've ever faced."

Paige's impact on Black baseball was unequaled. Buck O'Neil, the great

"IN MEXICO, I AM A MAN"

FOR TENS OF THOUSANDS OF BLACK FANS, Josh Gibson was the Negro National League's greatest star. And for one and a half seasons, he was also the greatest star of another league featuring highly talented ballplayers of color. It was the Mexican League, whose main sponsor was a wealthy businessman named Jorge Pasquel. To grow the league, Pasquel lured as many stars of the Negro Leagues to Mexico as he could, along with whatever white players he could recruit.

There's wide consensus that Josh Gibson, if permitted to play, would have been one of the greatest stars the major leagues had ever known. It's believed he may have died at a young age from the stress and depression of being barred from the major leagues.

The biggest of these lures was the size of the salaries Pasquel was offering Black ballplayers to defect, much higher than what the Negro Leagues paid. And for the Black athletes, enduring the daily trauma and pain of life in a largely segregated United States, there was another great enticement as well.

"It was the first time in my life that I felt free," Hall of Famer Monte Irvin later recalled. "We could go anywhere we wanted, eat anywhere we wanted, do anything we wanted . . . I owe that experience to Jorge Pasquel." All-star Negro League shortstop Willie Wells echoed these sentiments. "We live in the best hotels, we eat in the best restaurants," he declared. "We don't enjoy such privileges in the U.S. I didn't quit . . . and join some other team in the United States. I quit and left the country. I've found freedom and democracy here, something I never found in the United States. Here in Mexico, I am a man."

By 1940, there were sixty-three Negro players in the Mexican League, including Josh Gibson. Enticed by a huge salary offered by a team in the Venezuelan League, he had abruptly left the Grays, to whom he was under contract. When the Venezuelan League folded three quarters through the 1940 season, Gibson joined Veracruz in the Mexican League. Though he played only a quarter of a season for Veracruz that year, he nearly won the home run title while batting a lofty .467. In 1941, playing the full year for Veracruz, Gibson led his team to the Mexican League pennant by batting .374, and leading the league in home runs and runs batted in.

By 1942, however, he was back playing for the Homestead Grays, after its owner filed a lawsuit threatening to take away almost everything that Gibson owned if he did not return to the team that still had him under contract. His October 1941 return merited a screaming headline on the sports page of the *Pittsburgh Courier*.

But that did not discourage Pasquel. In the next five years, he not only recruited more major stars of the Negro Leagues but stars of the white major leagues as well. In his most aggressive moves, he offered huge salaries to major league ballplayers Joe DiMaggio, Ted Williams, and Bob Feller, but they all turned him down.

Jackie Robinson's signing with the Dodgers in 1945 as the first Black major leaguer marked the beginning of the end to Pasquel's ambitions. In the next decade, with the doors now open to what had, for so long, been an impossible dream, fifty-seven black ballplayers followed Robinson into the major leagues, making these leagues stronger than ever while diminishing the once lofty position of the Mexican League.

Josh Gibson (standing, far left) was a star of the Homestead Grays.

Black baseman and first African American coach in the major leagues, stated, "Satchel did to Black baseball what Ruth did to white baseball . . . This is the guy that the people wanted to see. And he never failed."

In 1941, Satchel Paige had just returned to the Black big leagues, after two years enmeshed in contract squabbles and plagued by an injury. He was said to have lost his fastball. During his time away, he developed a curveball and a few other alternative pitches, and then miraculously got his blinding fastball back too, adding to his mystique. So it's no surprise that fans clamored to see him in the all-star game, the biggest stage the Negro Leagues had to offer.

But sharing the mound on that blistering hot day would be Paige's fellow Kansas City Monarchs pitcher Hilton Smith, whose amazing career was often overshadowed by his teammate's. In order to draw the largest crowd possible, the Monarchs would frequently announce that Paige would be the game's starting pitcher. Start it he would, only to be relieved by Smith after one or two innings. Not only would Smith finish the game; he would finish it brilliantly as well.

According to Negro League historian Bob Kendrick, "The old-timers would all say that if you were going to hit anything, you better hit it off Satchel, because you weren't going to touch Hilton Smith." Smith and Paige's all-star game opponent Campanella put it simply. "My God," he declared, "you couldn't tell the difference."

As his Hall of Fame plaque reads, Smith was "a quiet but confident right hander whose devastating fastball complemented what many regard as the most sweeping curveball in Negro Leagues history." In each of the twelve seasons that Smith pitched for the Monarchs, he won more than twenty games. In 1941, he completed a record of 25-1. "I was pitching about four times a week," Smith explained, "because we were playing six or seven games a week, and we only carried about four

The most legendary of all Negro League baseball players was Satchel Paige. Polls show the public regards him as the most admired Negro League ballplayer of all time.

Baseball Hall of Fame pitcher Grover Cleveland Alexander stands on the mound and watches Satchel Paige of the New York Black Yankees at work.

pitchers . . . we didn't know what it was to relieve. When you went out there, you didn't look at the bullpen, you were expected to go the whole route." He was also an outstanding hitter. Often used as a pinch hitter, or as a third baseman or outfielder when he wasn't pitching, he compiled a lifetime batting average of close to .300.

Many probably thought they'd see Satchel start, but before the game, the *Defender* reported that West team manager Candy Jim Taylor planned to put Smith in first, flipping the usual script. The paper also advised fans, "Taylor is known for his cunning, and it would be a big surprise if Satchel were held to pitching the final three frames for the West." But Smith did indeed start.

Unfortunately, Smith had a tough time right from the get-go. He threw a strike on the game's first pitch, but immediately after that, the East's "Jimbo" Kimbro of the Birmingham Black Barons got to first due to a high throw from the West's second baseman. From there, Jimbo stole second, then went to third on a grounder before Leonard drove him in with a single to right. Then, yet another West miscue, a passed ball, gave the East a second run.

The fans began to boo the West for their errors, but they were playing in tough conditions. The *Afro-American* reported the "torrid 100-degree summer heat . . . saw a half-dozen players retire from the game because of the weather and kept fans overloading with soda pop and lemonade in a frantic effort to beat the heat."

In the second, the West answered with a run of its own, on a double from Ted Strong, and "it looked like we were going to see a whale of a ball game," the *Defender* reported. But then the roof fell in on the West all-stars in the fourth inning. And again, much of the damage was self-inflicted.

"The game itself was a demonstration of Eastern power and strategy over an impotent, ragged, although individually flashy crew of Westerns," wrote the *Star-News*.

The West gave up a couple of runs on a walk, two singles, and a sacrifice fly. The blunders continued until Buck Leonard stepped up to the plate.

Leonard "sent the crowd into a spell of pandemonium" by clouting a ball 360 feet into the right field stands, and with the score now 8-1, the game was pretty much decided. (Leonard won a tailor-made suit from a Chicago tailor for the homer.)

The East's impressive hitting compensated for its fielding, which, like the

The rosters of the Negro Leagues are filled with the names of thousands who never received anything close to the credit they deserved for their greatness. High on that list is Hilton Smith, who pitched for the Kansas City Monarchs from 1936 to 1950.

West's, was far from flawless, though not as costly in terms of runs. Between them, the teams made nine errors—leading the *Courier* to complain, "Ballplayers should realize the honor which is theirs in being chosen to represent their league in this annual classic. We contend that there is no reason for outfielders time and time again losing fly balls in the sun. Sun-glasses [sic] are a part of an outfielder's equipment, and we hold no brief for those players who don't have the tools of their profession."

"Errors are a part of baseball," the *Courier* went on, "and while we hated to see the game become so loose, we do know that the men who erred, erred trying. But those dropped fly balls—uh!"

Strangely enough, though, the game's Most Valuable Player Award was won by Roy Campanella on the strength of his defense. "Campanello [sic], playing his first year in the Classic, stole the show from his more experienced teammates with a brilliant and inspired display of heads up baseball. The big part in Roy's glory . . . was his grand fielding which stamped him as the favorite among the fans, and the newspapermen who voted him the most valuable award," raved the *Washington Afro-American*.

"Campanell[a] nailed Tommy Simpson in an attempted steal in the second; rifled a peg to Martinez in the 5th to make the only double play of the game, catching Cleveland at second after Horn fanned; went to the stands for Ted Strong's foul fly, and twice nipped fleet West players with speedy fielding of intended sacrifice bunts. In three of four of the cases mentioned Roy's brilliant work halted would be West rallies," the paper said.

The game was out of hand by the fifth inning, but there was one more thrill still remaining for the sweltering, record crowd. In the top of the eighth, his team trailing 8-3, the player so many had come to see took the hill at last. But Satchel Paige had to wait before throwing his first pitch.

"Every fan in the park wanted to see him and when he lazily dragged himself to the hill, he got an ovation usually reserved for Babe Ruth, Joe DiMaggio or Carl Hubble," the *Star-News* reported. After the crowd settled down, Paige proceeded to strike out the first two men he faced. Then he got Leonard to pop out to second. He faced four batters in the ninth, allowing no runs.

"If the West had any hero it had to be Satchel Paige, for Old Satch with his blinding speed ball and colorful antics, served to console West fans at a time when they were becoming disgusted with the wobbly defense of the American Leaguers (West)," wrote Art Carter of the *Washington Afro-American* after the game.

Aside from Paige's pitching, Leonard's hitting, and a "spectacular one-handed catch after [Monte] Irvin had leaped into the air" at third, the game on the field did not live up to the hype in 1941. Baseball purists were unhappy about the management of the West's roster, which Young claimed left the Eastern team saying, "They had a team on the bench which might have been able to beat us." But these were standard complaints of engaged observers about a thriving event, a sign more of health than of dysfunction. As a social happening, a platform for fun and enjoyment, it was everything the fans could have hoped for.

> ... PAIGE'S PITCHING, LEONARD'S HITTING, AND A "SPECTACULAR ONE-HANDED CATCH AFTER [MONTE] IRVIN HAD LEAPED INTO THE AIR" AT THIRD...

The game lasted until about 6:00 p.m., the temperature still in the eighties. The 50,000 attendees and the vendors and hucksters they attracted began the journey home. Meanwhile, half a world away, German forces surrounded

THE FIGHTING NINETY-SECOND

One of the most unique military divisions in World War II was the Ninety-Second Division of the United States' Fifth Army, one of three totally African American divisions and the only one to serve in combat. Known commonly as the "Buffalo Soldiers," the division trained at Fort Huachuca, Arizona, and was then deployed to Italy to join in the ongoing assault against enemy forces in the Alps mountains.

The all-Black division spent August 1944 to the end of the war in May 1945 serving with extraordinary bravery and distinction. During that time, it repeatedly advanced and captured more than 20,000 German prisoners, all despite suffering thousands of casualties.

For their amazing accomplishments, members of the "Fighting Ninety-Second" earned more than 12,000 decorations and citations including the Congressional Medal of Honor. One of the recipients of the military's highest award was First Lieutenant Vernon Baker who, on April 5 and April 6, 1945, demonstrated amazing bravery and leadership. When his company was undergoing enemy fire, Baker crawled to a different position and destroyed a German machine gun nest, killing three of the enemy. He then attacked a German observation post, killing two soldiers and putting the key post out of commission. He was still not done. With the help of one of his men, he attacked two other machine gun nests, killing four more of the enemy in the process. The very next night, Lieutenant Baker led a successful Ninety-Second Division advance through enemy minefields amid heavy fire.

The other member of the Ninety-Second to receive the Medal of Honor was First Lieutenant John R. Fox who, on December 26, 1944, in Italy's Serchio River Valley sacrificed his own life to delay advancing enemy forces until reinforcements arrived to save his division.

When World War II ended, fifty-three men from the Ninety-Second were still missing. Despite intense searches, only three of them have ever been found, adding to the extraordinary sacrifices the Black division made on behalf of a nation that still treated them as second-class citizens.

Members of the all-Black 92nd Infantry Division pursue retreating German Troops through the Po Valley in Italy.

the Red Army and took 100,000 Russian soldiers prisoner. The crowds would return to the East-West game in 1942, but it would be in a wartime America on a military footing, and the social forces that would destroy the "color line" would be at work as Black people by the millions served their country.

Monte Irvin, who had had two hits in the 1941 game, anticipated what may well have been the most important contribution not only of the annual contest but of Black baseball itself. "More than anything else," he wrote, "[the East-West All-Star Game] gave black Americans hope all across the country. . . . They said if these players can succeed under these very difficult conditions, then maybe we can too."

Indeed, Black baseball, like the white majors, provided Americans with a sorely needed diversion in 1941. It was a source of pride, community, and hope during trying times. But in baseball and in the country, historic changes were just around the corner.

These changes would affect each 1941 all-star differently.

Buck Leonard was of an age group that just missed out on gaining full recognition and respect for their greatness during their playing days. Offered a major league contract by the Browns in 1952, Leonard declined. "I knew I was over the hill," he wrote later. "I didn't try to fool myself."

Campanella was young enough that he was able to rise to glory as a full major leaguer. He began playing for the Brooklyn Dodgers in 1948, where he and pitcher Don Newcombe joined Jackie Robinson as some of the earliest, bravest racial pioneers in baseball. He won a World Series with the Dodgers in 1955 and was MVP of the National League three times in the 1950s. By then, he was a nationally known superstar. But even more than his bravery in the face of bigotry, more than his tremendous hustle and skill, Campanella is admired for how he responded after his career ended horribly. In January 1958, an automobile accident left him a quadriplegic. But

> **IT WAS A SOURCE OF PRIDE, COMMUNITY, AND HOPE DURING TRYING TIMES.**

An important first in the history of the Major League All Star Game: the first Negro League players ever selected pose together. They are, left to right: Roy Campanella, Larry Doby, Don Newcombe, and Jackie Robinson.

"Campy" displayed the toughness and winning attitude that had made him such a fearsome force on the diamond, spending decades as a Dodgers scout and an advocate for people with disabilities.

"We're a rugged breed, us quads," he wrote in his autobiography, in a paragraph capturing the essence of his special greatness. "If we weren't we wouldn't be around today. Yes, we're a rugged breed, and in many ways we've been blessed with a savvy and spirit that isn't given to everybody."

Like Campanella, Monte Irvin was young enough that he was able to cross the color barrier and get a measure of recognition and satisfaction. As a member of the integrated New York Giants, Irvin played in two World Series, made it to the Hall of Fame, and was a guide and role model for Giants immortal Willie Mays when Mays broke in in the early 1950s.

Hilton Smith's baseball career was not only brilliant but long as well. He was still pitching in 1947 when Jackie Robinson broke the color line with the Brooklyn Dodgers. By that time, Smith had beaten major league teams six

The first all-Black outfield in Major League Baseball was featured in the 1951 World Series with the New York Giants—left to right: Monte Irvin, Willie Mays, and Hank Thompson.

out of the seven times he had pitched against them. But when the Dodgers made him an offer, he realized that his best years were behind him and turned them down. Almost everyone who had ever seen him pitch had no doubt that if his chance had come sooner, Hilton Smith would have been one of the greatest stars of the major leagues.

Satchel Paige played in the Negro Leagues until he was forty-two, when in 1948 Cleveland Indians owner Bill Veeck signed him to a major league deal. He pitched so well that year, including a World Series appearance, that there was talk of naming him Rookie of the Year, an idea he found distasteful. Of all the great Black players, Paige is still the best known, for both his fifty years of incredible-but-true exploits on the field, and also his captivating flamboyance and such observations as, "If someone asked you how old you were and you didn't know your age, how old would you think you were?"

In 1941, Ted Williams had unwittingly excluded Black players from his definition of the "best of the best." But when he was inducted into the Hall of Fame in 1966, Williams used his national stage to call for their inclusion, in the Hall, and in America's consciousness.

He'd long since learned to recognize the greatness of his Black peers.

Some twenty-five years later, with the nation gripped by civil rights conflict, Williams made sure to tell the audience at his induction ceremony: "I hope someday Satchel Paige and Josh Gibson will be voted into the Hall of Fame as symbols of the great Negro players who are not here only because they weren't given the chance." No one in the audience applauded. But the words did capture attention beyond Cooperstown. Ever reluctant to do the right thing, baseball took five more years to permit the induction of Paige and Gibson, but it did happen.

Paige and Gibson were followed by thirty-five other Black stars over time, including Buck Leonard in 1972 and Monte Irvin in 1973. Addressing the Hall of Fame crowd the day he was inducted, Irvin said, "I played in the Bus Leagues for many years—overworked, underpaid, but somehow now this does not seem to be in vain. And I hope my induction will help to ease the pain of all those players who never got a chance to play in the majors."

One of them, Cool Papa Bell, was happy to be inducted in 1974, but did express some of the pain as well: "They say we was born too soon, but it wasn't that," he said. "They opened the doors too late."

It wasn't until 1962 that former Negro League players were admitted into baseball's Hall of Fame. Here, James "Cool Papa" Bell, who many regard as the fastest man to play the game, holds a special bat to celebrate his admission.

TWENTY-FIVE CENTS

NEW YORK YANKEES

BROOKLYN DODGERS

1941 WORLD SERIES

5

THE WORLD SERIES

IT WAS THE FIRST DAY OF OCTOBER, and the 1941 World Series between the powerhouse New York Yankees and the underdog Brooklyn Dodgers was about to begin. And, just as a truly remarkable season had captured hearts and minds around the country, Americans were hopeful that at a time when world news was becoming more ominous than ever the Series would provide as much excitement and sorely needed diversion as had the regular season.

"Blasé New York, which long since had come to regard itself as fully capable of taking a World Series right in stride, found itself gripped last night in a baseball fever which threatened to reach alarming proportions," reported *The New York Times* on its front page the day the Series opened. And the New York *Daily News* captured the mood of long-suffering Dodgers fans: "Brooklyn awoke breathless this morning, gulped breakfast into a nervous stomach and impatiently awaited greater glory."

The two teams were a study in contrasts.

The Yankees were in the midst of the greatest dynasty the baseball world had ever

The front cover of the official program for the 1941 World Series.

known. They had won the American League pennant in four consecutive seasons from 1936–1939. In three of those four seasons, their win total exceeded the second-place team's by double digits. In this era, they notched equally remarkable home run totals, including a major league record 182 round-trippers in 1936.

Their dominance extended to the World Series, which they won four straight times from 1936 through 1939. (No other team had ever won more than two Fall Classics in a row.) And they had done it in overpowering fashion, outscoring their opponents by a huge number of runs in many of these games. All told, as they entered the 1941 Fall Classic, the Yankees had won thirteen of their last fourteen World Series games and twenty-eight of their last thirty-one.

They were not only talented and powerful; the 1941 Yankees were also a team on a mission. Although they had been heavily favored to win it all again in 1940, for reasons they and their fans were still trying to figure out, they had finished second to the Detroit Tigers in the regular season, missing the Fall Classic altogether. So in 1941, they had played with a vengeance. Joe DiMaggio's fifty-six-game hitting streak set the tone, but the whole team got in on the act. Each of their three outfielders—Joe DiMaggio, Tommy Henrich, and Charlie Keller—had hit thirty or more home runs during the season. Second baseman Joe Gordon had added twenty-four more. The Yankees lineup also included future Hall of Famers catcher Bill Dickey, shortstop Phil Rizzuto, and pitchers Red Ruffing and Lefty Gomez. Holding a twenty-game lead over the then second-place Chicago White Sox, they clinched the pennant on September 4, the earliest ever in the American League, and won the pennant by seventeen games.

The Dodgers, on the other hand, had a less impressive track record. They

The 1941 New York Yankees were a powerful team. These four Bronx Bombers alone (left to right: Tommy Henrich, Joe DiMaggio, Charlie Keller, and Joe Gordon) were among the most feared hitters in baseball.

had not won a National League pennant since 1920 and had never won a World Series. Their promising 1920 season had been followed by almost twenty years of what one sportswriter called "unalloyed mediocrity" that included two seventh-place finishes in an eight-team league and then ten sixth-place finishes.

It was not just the fact that they lost so often, but the *way* they lost that had earned them the name "Daffiness Boys." Some of the "bonehead plays" they made became part of baseball legend. There was, for example, the time that a Dodger outfielder got hit on the head with a fly ball because he was in the midst of arguing with a fan in the stands, or the time that three Dodgers slid into third base at the same time. The poster boy of the Dodgers' ineptitude

Both the Yankees and the Dodgers entered the World Series featuring an outstanding rookie. For the Dodgers it was the slick-fielding Pee Wee Reese.

The Yankees' star rookie was scrappy, hard-hitting Phil Rizzuto.

was outfielder Babe Herman who, for reasons known only to him, carried lit cigars in his pockets. A writer for *Collier's* magazine gave a vivid account of Herman's fielding abilities. "It was an even bet," the writer stated, "that Babe would catch a fly ball or get killed by it. His general practice was to run up when the ball was hit and then turn and run back and then circle around uncertainly. All this time the ball was descending, the spectators were petrified with fear, and Mr. Herman was chewing gum unconcerned. At the proper moment he stuck out his glove. If he found the ball there he was greatly surprised and very happy."

And yet year after year, the people in Brooklyn lived in hope. "Wait till next year" became their slogan. But to outsiders, "the Dodgers," wrote author Robert Creamer, were nothing more than "a joke team from a joke town."

That all began to change in 1938, when the Dodgers hired Larry MacPhail away from the Cincinnati Reds to be their new executive vice president. An often argumentative man, prone to rapid changes of mood, he was nonetheless a skilled and imaginative executive. While with the Reds, MacPhail had introduced night baseball to the major leagues, and he had also made the club a pioneer in radio broadcasts of their games.

He took charge of the Dodgers at the lowest point in their history. Not only were they playing poorly, but they were also more than a million dollars in debt. Things had gotten so bad that the office telephones had been disconnected because the phone bill had not been paid.

Despite his erratic behavior, MacPhail could be both charming and persuasive. He began his transformation of the Dodgers by enticing banks to lend the team, in as poor shape as it was, a great deal of money. Then he set about rebuilding. With an eye to the future, he added six additional minor league teams to the Dodgers' farm system and signed working agreements with six others. He also hired fifteen new scouts and sent them out looking for prospects. Then he turned his attention to the team itself.

He began by hiring Leo Durocher, the Dodgers shortstop, to be the team's manager. Like MacPhail, Durocher was driven by a fierce desire to win, and both men had similarly strong personalities. During the four years they worked together, MacPhail fired Durocher at least sixty times, only to rehire him the next day. As one sports reporter put it, "they loathed each other, yet respected one another enough to co-exist."

In 1939, aided by Durocher, MacPhail set out to change almost the entire Dodgers roster. Through trades, purchases, shrewd dealings, and, most of all, a willingness to take risks, he put together a brand-new and highly talented team—a mix of high-priced veterans, promising young talents, and flat-out bargains. Mostly, he took a chance on players who had been discarded by other teams who, he felt, had the potential to find new life with the Dodgers. By 1941, all eight of the Dodgers starting players and all five of their starting pitchers had begun their baseball careers with other major league organizations.

At the same time he was turning the hapless Dodgers into a pennant

The most fiery of all the Dodgers was their manager, Leo Durocher, shown here arguing with an umpire during the 1941 World Series.

contender, MacPhail also increased revenue by bringing more fans into the ballpark. He had initiated radio broadcasts of Reds games, and he did the same thing when he took over the Dodgers, bringing young announcer Red Barber with him from Cincinnati to Brooklyn. Later in his career, Barber would explain why at the time broadcasting the games was such a bold move.

"Anything new has to establish itself and gain its own credentials," Barber stated. "When radio came along and began to broadcast some baseball games, some of the entrenched conservative owners said, 'Wait a minute. Why give away something that you're trying to sell for your living, to try and keep your enterprise afloat?' And especially on days of threatening weather when people would say, 'well it looks like it may rain. I'll just listen [to the game] on the radio. I won't go.' They did not realize at the time the beneficial effect of radio, that it would be making families of fans. And so it got so bad that after the season of 1933, baseball considered banning all radio play-by-play . . .

Dodger hitting leaders included (left to right) Arky Vaughn, Dolph Camilli, Billy Herman, and Pee Wee Reese.

MacPhail broke [the radio ban] in Brooklyn in thirty-nine and from that time on there's been no question. Radio, television, more fans, more money."

On June 15, 1938, MacPhail brought night baseball to Brooklyn. This first night game in the huge New York area attracted a crowd of almost 39,000 people, and they witnessed a historic game: Johnny Vander Meer of the visiting Reds pitched his second consecutive no-hitter, something that has never been duplicated in the major leagues.

Gradually, all the moves and all the innovations that MacPhail put into place began to pay off. After years of foundering near the bottom of the standings, the Dodgers became serious contenders for the pennant. "In 1939 you could see it coming," recalled one

One of the Dodgers' brightest stars was the multitalented Pete Reiser, shown sliding home in a game.

fan. "Third place, then second place in 1940, and you knew that in 1941 they were finally going to do it."

Truth be told, it was not that simple. While the Yankees quickly amassed a comfortable lead in the American League thanks to DiMaggio's incredible season, the 1941 National League pennant contest was a neck-and-neck race between two teams and two teams only—the Dodgers and the St. Louis Cardinals. Aside from nine days at the beginning of the season, either the Dodgers or the Cardinals were in first place, or the two were tied. A crucial late-season series with the Cardinals finally gave the Dodgers the pennant, which they won by two and a half games.

For the Dodgers, it was their greatest season ever, setting a team record

THE BIRTH OF NIGHT BASEBALL

Like catchers' shin guards and batting helmets, night baseball was introduced to the game by the barnstorming Black ball clubs. The person most responsible for its introduction was Kansas City Monarchs owner JL Wilkinson.

In 1929, Wilkinson mortgaged everything he owned to commission an Omaha company to construct a set of fifty-foot portable generator-powered light towers.

On April 28, 1930, the Monarchs staged their first night game, and soon Wilkinson's barnstorming ball club was playing games under the lights both in their home ballpark and on the road. "Wilkinson wasn't doing it for innovation," stated Negro Leagues Baseball Museum president Bob Kendrick. "He was doing it for survival."

And he was looking for a way to get more working-class fans into the ballpark. Wilkinson had found that hundreds of people who wanted to see baseball games could not on account of work schedules.

As with so many innovations in the game, Wilkinson's plan was met with scores of naysayers explaining why night baseball would never succeed. "The night air is not like the day air," proclaimed the *Sporting News*, "and the man who goes to baseball after he has eaten a hearty meal is apt to have indigestion if he is nervous and excited."

In its first stages, night baseball was far from perfect. Negro League star third baseman Judy Johnson commented on the inadequacy of the earliest lights, explaining, "I couldn't see the outfielders out there. If the ball went above the lights, you'd have to watch out it didn't hit you in the head." Despite these flaws, night baseball was adopted by a number of Black barnstorming teams, which quickly discovered that holiday games at night drew more fans than ever before. Writing about a game between two Black teams at Pittsburgh's Forbes Field, white sportswriter Ralph Davis stated that "the scene was a revelation to many doubting Thomases who went to scoff and left the field declaring that perhaps after all, the national pastime, if it ever has to be saved, will find night performances its savior."

Thanks to the example set by the Negro League teams, minor league teams around the country erected lights, with several of them finding that playing at night doubled their attendance. By the time the Reds met the Phillies at Crosley Field on May 24, 1935, the major leagues were more than ready for baseball under the lights.

The introduction of night baseball in the 1930s revolutionized the game.

of one hundred wins. Dolph Camilli, who led the league in home runs with thirty-four and in runs batted in with 120, was named the National League's most valuable player. Pete Reiser led the league in hitting (.343) and in doubles and triples. Whitlow Wyatt and Kirby Higbe each won twenty-two games. "No one man carried our club," said Camilli, "we all had great years."

The Dodgers' rise from the ashes was uniquely captivating. DiMaggio's streak had held the nation's attention for some two months in the middle of the season. Ted Williams had captured the headlines at the end of the campaign. The Negro Leagues East-West All-Star Game had drawn record crowds on one singular, sweltering day in July. With their climb to the pennant, the Dodgers stole the minds and hearts of the baseball world for the entire season. What made the Dodgers special in 1941 wasn't just their winning record, but also the uniquely entertaining brand of baseball they displayed. And just as entertaining as the team on the field, if not more so, was the Dodgers' fandom.

> **... THE DODGERS HAD THE MOST LOYAL, VOCAL, AND FERVENT FANS ANYWHERE.**

Despite their long years of futility on the field, the Dodgers had the most loyal, vocal, and fervent fans anywhere. Part of it had to do with their ballpark Ebbets Field, the smallest and most intimate park in the National League. "If you were sitting in a box seat at first base," stated Red Barber, "you could almost see the fingers on Dolph Camilli's hand. You could hear what the players said if you had a seat along first base. If you were in the stands at Ebbets Field, you were practically in the ball game."

The intimacy of the ballpark led to an intimacy between the fans and the ballplayers. Before each game, fans would line up along the railing of the stands and players would walk past and shake everybody's hand and sign autographs, and talk about that afternoon's game. When a player had a birthday, he could expect birthday cakes and perhaps some presents from fans waiting for him in the locker room after the game.

Ebbets Field was arguably the noisiest ballpark in America, and among the many contributors to the constant racket was a brass band made up of amateur musicians. Formed in response to the excitement engendered by the 1941 pennant drive, the five members of what Red Barber quickly dubbed "the Dodger Sym-phony" would play and dance on top of the dugout and wander through the stands, adding to the noise and serenading the fans. When the umpires went on the field, they played "Three Blind Mice." When an opposing pitcher was knocked out of the game, they made fun of him by playing a funeral dirge.

Adding to it all was the Dodgers public address announcer Tex Rickard, a man with his own understanding of the English language. During one game he announced, "A little boy has been found lost." During another he barked, "Would the fans along the railing in left field please remove their clothes?"

The 1941 World Series began on October 1. Reflecting how essential the joy of baseball was to the nation as it moved closer and closer to going to war, more than 68,000 fans poured into Yankee Stadium.

And in this first game, "Brooklyn's dazzling Dodgers," reported *The New York Times*, "whose dramatic National League pennant Victory touched a new baseball high for mass hysteria, advanced upon the Yankee Stadium yesterday, brought with them legions of devout followers who helped set a World Series attendance record of 68,540 and then unhappily [by the score of 3-2] got themselves lost in the vastness of the situation." It was obvious to everyone that the Yankees were going to take the series easily.

But the next day, with Yankee Stadium again filled to overflowing, the Dodgers showed they were still in the fight, registering a 3-2 win. For the first time in the series, tempers flared when, in an attempt to break up a double play, Dodgers catcher Mickey Owen knocked down

While the 1941 World Series excitement was engrossing fans, America's entry into a world war was drawing closer as ships from various nations were being sunk by German submarines.

THE GREATEST FANS IN BASEBALL

A NUMBER OF THE DODGER FANS became almost as famous as the players on the field. "Eddie Battan," said Red Barber, "was a real fan of Brooklyn. He had a little piercing whistle, and he would whistle at a ballplayer, say a pitcher, like [Whitlow] Wyatt, and he would start calling 'Whit,' and he would keep calling 'Whit' at the top of his voice until Wyatt took off his cap and bowed to Eddie Battan."

And then there was Jack Pierce, best known for continually screaming, "Cooooooooookie, Coooooookie, Coooooookie," in praise of his hero, Dodgers third baseman Cookie Lavagetto. Pierce bought three seats for every home game—one for himself, one for a friend, and one for the multitude of balloons that became his trademark.

The most famous and noisiest fan of all was a woman named Hilda Chester who with her cowbells and special antics became not only the Dodgers' "acknowledged" superfan but also the most famous in all baseball. The *Sporting News* called her "the undisputed Queen of the Bleachers, the spirit of Brooklyn, the Bell of Ebbets Field."

Dodger fans who had waited twenty-one years for their beloved "bums" to win the National League pennant went wild when it finally happened in 1941.

Sportswriter Dan Daniel dubbed her "the Brooklyn Foghorn." The *Los Angeles Times* described her most vividly of all as "a woman who would scream like a fishmonger at players and managers and lead fans in snake dances through the aisles." Author Peter Golenbock correctly labeled her "the most famous of the Dodger fans—perhaps the most famous fan in baseball history."

She had the loudest voice in the ballpark, but when, after suffering a mild heart attack, her doctor forbade her to yell, the Dodgers players presented her with the first of the large cowbells that became her trademark and call to arms. "That bell," wrote the *Sporting News*, "is an important part of Hilda's life. She rings it to signal every vital turn of Dodger affairs."

Chester became so much a part of Dodger life that on one occasion she actually influenced the flow of the game. From her center field bleacher seat, she threw down a note to Pete Reiser, asking him to take it to manager Leo Durocher in the dugout. The note said that the Dodgers pitcher was tiring and should be taken out. Thinking that the note came from general manager Larry MacPhail, Durocher brought in a reliever. It was not until after the game that he found out that the note had come from Hilda.

Before her career as a superfan was over, Hilda became almost as big of a celebrity as some of the players. She was a guest on several television talk shows and appeared in several scenes in the motion pictures *The Jackie Robinson Story* and *Brooklyn, I Love You*. In 1955, in a major event, the Dodgers honored their all-time all-star team. Only one non-player made the roster: Hilda Chester.

The Dodger faithful wait overnight in line at Ebbets Field for tickets to the 1941 World Series.

As he had been throughout the season, Joe DiMaggio was one of the standouts of the 1941 World Series.

Advances in photography and television brought the action of the 1941 World Series closer to more fans than ever before. In this photograph, taken during the second game of the series, Yankee pitcher Spud Chandler is thrown out at third base.

Yankees shortstop Phil Rizzuto. Rizzuto threw to first, then angrily started toward Owen. Teammate Tommy Heinrich stepped in front of Rizzuto, heading off a brawl, but the Yankees were fighting mad. "[Owen] must have gone 10 feet out of his way to smack Phil down," a usually calm Joe DiMaggio said after the game.

On October 4, 1941, the Brooklyn Dodgers hosted their first World Series game in twenty-one years. For seven innings, it was a brilliant, scoreless pitching duel, until the Yankees' Marius Russo hit a vicious line drive that struck the Dodgers' pitcher "Fat Freddie" Fitzsimmons just above his left kneecap. The ball was hit so hard that it ricocheted straight into shortstop Pee Wee Reese's glove without touching the ground. Fitzsimmons, who had held the Yankees completely in check thus far, had to be helped off the field.

The Dodgers brought in Hugh Casey in relief, but in the eighth inning, the Yankees greeted the usually rock-solid reliever with four straight hits resulting in the first two runs of the game. The Dodgers scored a run of their own in the bottom of the eighth, but it was not enough. Game three went to the Yankees, 2-1.

The New York Times

108 ♦ BASEBALL'S SHINING SEASON

summed up the situation tartly the next morning: "After a lapse of 21 years, they brought the World Series to Brooklyn yesterday. But, in an unguarded moment, they also let in the Yankees, and the mistake was one which eventually proved fatal . . . Joe McCarthy's Bronx Bombers, by capturing this third game of the current World Series, are once again in front, exuding their familiar aura of invincibility."

WITH THE YANKEES LEADING two games to one, game four became absolutely crucial for the Dodgers. But the contest got off to a rocky start for them, and by the fifth inning, the Yankees were leading 3-2. Once again Durocher brought in Hugh Casey in relief. This time, Casey, who had taken a beating in the press for having lost game three after "Fat Freddie" Fitzsimmons had pitched so brilliantly, was up to the task, holding further runs at bay.

Most cameras were still bulky and cumbersome, but in 1941 more photographers than ever covered the World Series.

The usually raucous Dodgers fans became absolutely delirious when, in the bottom of the fifth, Pete Reiser's two-run homer gave the Dodgers a 4-3 lead. That score held up to the ninth: the Dodgers needed just three final outs to claim a 4-3 victory and tie the series at two games apiece.

The Yankees' first batter in the top of the ninth was Johnny Sturm, and Casey retired him on a ground ball to the infield. The next batter, hard-hitting Red Rolfe, had no better luck. Up third was Tommy Henrich who had gone zero for four for the day. With Dodgers fans on their feet screaming for the final out, Casey worked the count to 3-2. Catcher Mickey Owen called for Casey to throw his curveball, one of the most effective pitches in all of baseball.

Throw it he did, and Henrich swung and missed. The game was over. The Dodgers had tied the series.

But—not really. Although police officers had already stepped onto the field to perform postgame crowd control, the ball was still live: it kicked off catcher Owen's glove and rolled to the backstop. Realizing what had happened, Henrich raced to first base, arriving safely before Owen could even make a throw. "I knew that Casey had a very good high curve, and that's a pitch that always gave me trouble," Henrich later recounted. "Couldn't hit it for the life of me. And so here I am with two strikes against me and here it comes. It was a beauty, one of the best and craziest curveballs I've ever seen. It was definitely not a spitter as some people have claimed. I thought it was going to be a strike so I started my swing. And then that pitch broke sharply down. I tried to hold up, but it was too late. I'd committed myself. The funny thing is that even in that instant, while I was swinging, I thought to myself that if I'm having this much trouble with the pitch, maybe Mickey Owen is too. So I looked around behind me after I missed the ball and I saw the ball heading for the backstop. I set sail for first. I'll admit I was as surprised as anyone in the park."

Mickey Owen, who had amassed 508 putouts and assists that season without a single error, took full blame for the

The Dodgers boasted the most demonstrative fans in the world. Here one of them, sporting both a bullhorn and an umbrella, cheers them on during the opening game of the 1941 World Series.

miscue. "It was all my fault," he later said. "It wasn't a strike. It was a great breaking curve that I should have had. But I guess the ball hit the side of my glove. It got away from me and by the time I got hold of it, near the corner of the Brooklyn dugout, I couldn't have thrown anybody out at first."

The Dodgers were still a run ahead and still one out away from victory. But the crowd had gone silent. Dodgers fans were all too accustomed to things turning against them. Robert Angell, who would become one of baseball's greatest writers, wrote, "The minute that happened, as soon as Owen dropped the ball, you knew somehow the Yankees were going to win."

Unfortunately for the Dodgers, he was right. The next batter, Joe DiMaggio, singled to left. Then Charlie Keller doubled to right, scoring both Henrich and DiMaggio. A walk from Bill Dickey and a Joe Gordon

One of the most famous moments in World Series history: Brooklyn catcher Mickey Owen drops the ball after his pitcher had struck out Yankees batter Tommy Henrich.

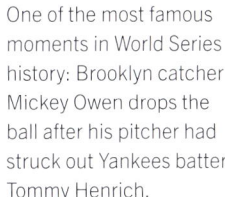

In this dramatic photograph, Henrich heads for first base as Owen feverishly chases the ball.

The 1941 World Series was hard played and bitterly fought. This was the scene at Ebbets Field when Joe DiMaggio and Whitlow Wyatt came close to trading blows.

double rounded out this astonishing comeback. The Yankees, one out away from defeat, had scored four runs and taken a decisive lead. The Dodgers, as stunned as their fans, could not recover from such a botched game. In the bottom of the ninth, they went out in order and lost the contest 7-4. Years later, Mickey Owen reflected upon that game, when the most famous "third strike" in history got away from him. "I'm only sorry about one thing," he said. "I should have called time and stopped the game, giving Casey and myself a chance to get over the shock. I've always kicked myself for not doing that."

In the visitors' clubhouse, the Yankees were jubilant, although Joe DiMaggio hadn't forgotten Owen's rough slide in game two, and let the reporters know. "No, we're not sorry for [Owen]," the normally mild-mannered DiMaggio said. "I'm glad it was him."

At the other end of the spectrum were the woebegone Dodgers fans still sitting in their Ebbets Field seats, contemplating the disaster long after the final out. One of them disparagingly asked a *Times* reporter, "Are the Bums REALLY bums?"

After all that had transpired in that one-of-a-kind baseball season, all the greatness baseball fans had witnessed over that year, it would take a uniquely special World Series to leave a lasting impression on Americans, with so much else occupying their minds in the fall of 1941. But sure enough, baseball had managed to deliver something nobody had expected.

The next day the Yankees' Ernie "Tiny" Bonham finished the Dodgers off by tossing a four-hitter. Ironically the key hit in the clinching victory was a homer struck by Tommy Henrich. But players on both the teams knew that the series had been decided the day before. "It could only happen in Brooklyn," wrote the sports scribe Red Smith. "Nowhere else in this broad untidy universe, not in Bedlam nor in Babel nor in the remotest psychopathic ward . . . only in the ancestral home of the Dodgers . . . could a man win a World Series game by striking out."

The 1941 World Series Champions, the New York Yankees, pose for their team portrait. Reflective of the role that the ever-expanding war played in the 1941 season was the presence of three army officers in the picture.

THE WORLD SERIES ◆ 113

6

BASEBALL GOES TO WAR

THE WAR HAD LOOMED OVER the entire 1941 season, but its largest impact came two months after the Yankees notched their decisive World Series victory. On December 7, 1941, in a surprise attack, hundreds of Japanese fighter planes descended on the US naval base at Pearl Harbor near Honolulu, Hawai'i. Nineteen American warships, including eight battleships, and 188 airplanes were destroyed. More than 2,400 Americans, including civilians, died in the attack, and another one thousand people were wounded. As had been so long anticipated and feared, the United States was at war.

World War II had a devastating effect on almost every aspect of American life, and major league baseball was no exception. More than five hundred major leaguers, including many of the game's biggest stars, were either drafted into the military or, particularly after Pearl Harbor, voluntarily enlisted in the armed forces.

Hank Greenberg, who had been the first major league star to be drafted back in May 1941, once again made headlines. He had just

The December 7, 1941, Japanese attack on Pearl Harbor launched the United States into the largest war in its history.

In a most haunting photograph, sailors play ball on the vast deck of the doomed battleship USS *Arizona*.

been released from service on December 5, 1941, because, at thirty years old, he was beyond draft age. When, only two days later, Japan carried out its raid on Pearl Harbor, he rushed to reenlist. "We are in trouble," he declared "and there is only one thing for me to do—return to the service. This one thing doubtless means I am finished with baseball and it would be silly for me to say I do not leave it without a pang. But all of us are confronted with a terrible task—the defense of our country and the fight for our lives."

With so many major and minor leaguers off to the war, people inside and outside the game began to ask whether baseball should close down in solidarity.

Baseball was so important to so many Americans that letters poured into the country's newspapers and magazines pleading that the nation's pastime go on. In Plumas County, California, the *Feather River Bulletin* went even further, declaring, "Baseball is more than a national game. It is America's anchor. It keeps the ship of state fast to its moorings in a balanced life."

Despite these pleas, baseball commissioner Judge Kenesaw Mountain Landis was uncertain how best to proceed. For guidance, he turned to the nation's leader, President Franklin D. Roosevelt. "Baseball," he wrote to the chief executive, "is about to adopt schedules, sign players, make vast commitments, go to training camp. What do you want us to do?" Landis then listed several options ranging from closing down completely to carrying out business as usual.

President Franklin D. Roosevelt was a huge baseball fan. "Roosevelt enjoys himself at a ballgame as much as a kid on Christmas morning," author Harold Burr wrote in his 1939 book, *Baseball*. "Once in his field box, the President . . . gets right into the spirit of the game, munches peanuts, applauds good plays and chuckles over bad ones."

PEARL HARBOR

Pearl Harbor is a lagoon harbor on the island of Oahu, Hawai'i, west of Honolulu. Once a thriving whaling center, it was acquired by the United States when the country annexed Hawai'i following the Spanish American War in 1898. In October 1941, as the Dodgers and the Yankees clashed in the World Series, few Americans had ever heard of Pearl Harbor let alone knew where it was or that it was the home base of the US Pacific fleet.

In hindsight, the Japanese assault on Pearl Harbor, an event that brought America into World War II, was the inevitable result of tensions that had been brewing for almost ten years. The militant Japanese government had aimed to become a world power, but as an island nation, Japan was limited both in size and resources. In order to begin changing that situation, the country, starting in the 1930s, launched a series of invasions of China along with a takeover of resources-rich Manchuria.

Convinced that this was the beginning of a military-led policy of global expansion, the US government invoked a series of economic sanctions against Japan including trade embargoes on oil, scrap metal, and other vital goods. The situation got more tense in November 1940, when Japan signed a military alliance with both Germany and Italy, the two leading countries at war with the Allies.

For the next year, the United States and Japan held almost nonstop negotiations, with the United States hoping that their sanctions and other threats would keep Japan at bay. But even while the two sides were meeting, Japanese aircraft carriers, carrying bomb and torpedo-launching planes, were heading toward Pearl Harbor. Only two months earlier, Americans had been focusing their attention on home runs and double plays. But on December 7, 1941, they were forced to turn their focus to matters no less serious than the future of civilization.

President Franklin D. Roosevelt opens the baseball season by throwing out the first pitch.

Within twenty-four hours of hearing from Commissioner Landis, Roosevelt responded with what has become known as the "Green Light Letter." "I honestly feel," he informed Landis, "that it would be best for the country to keep baseball going. Everybody will work longer hours and harder than ever before. And that means that they ought to have a chance . . . for taking their minds off their work even more than before. As for the players themselves," the president continued, "I know you agree with me that individual players who are of active military or naval age should go, without question, into the services. Even if the actual quality of the teams is lowered by greater use of older players, this will not dampen the popularity of the sport."

Thanks to President Roosevelt and his "Green Light Letter," and much to the relief of baseball fans everywhere, Major League Baseball played a full schedule of games throughout the war years. It would be a different brand of baseball, but it would be baseball nonetheless.

Meanwhile, the exodus of newly enlisted players set off a mad scramble as team owners frantically sought replacements for their absent stars.

The Dodgers signed forty-two-year-old Babe Herman, who had been out of baseball since 1937. Forty-one-year-old Paul Waner, a onetime Pittsburgh Pirates powerhouse, joined the Yankees. Pepper Martin, the star of the 1931 World Series, came back to the Cardinals four years after having last played for them. Ben Chapman, who had been an outfielder with the Yankees in the 1930s, reinvented himself and became a starting pitcher, first for the Dodgers and then for the Phillies. Thirty-eight-year-old Dodgers manager Leo Durocher, outraged at the poor play of his depleted infielders, reactivated himself as a second baseman, taking on an unusual player-manager role.

At the other end of the age scale, sixteen-year-old Nelson Fox went to spring training with the 1944 Philadelphia Athletics. Sixteen-year-old Carl Scheib progressed even further, making the team and pitching games in relief for the A's. And the Dodgers added sixteen-year-old shortstop Tommy Brown to their roster. The Cincinnati Reds, however, outdid them all by sending fifteen-year-old high school junior Joe Nuxhall to the mound against the St. Louis Cardinals. Nuxhall successfully retired two batters, but also gave up two hits, five walks, and five runs before being taken out of the game.

While a new crop of players got their time to shine during these four wartime baseball seasons, the loss of star power was unmistakable. Nothing illustrates the uniqueness of these four seasons quite like the story of the 1944 St. Louis Browns.

The St. Louis Browns had never won anything and had never been to the World Series. Not only were they bad, but in one regard they were unlucky as well. When the 1941 season ended, they were preparing to move their franchise to Los Angeles where they were certain to draw more fans. Just as they were about to do

The shortage of qualified major leaguers due to the war led the Cincinnati Reds to play the youngest player ever in a major league ball club: fifteen-year-old Joe Nuxhall.

MAJOR-LEAGUE WAR HEROES

MORE THAN FIVE HUNDRED Major League Baseball players served in the United States armed forces during Work War II. Some of them saw combat, some of them played supporting roles, and some made the ultimate sacrifice. And four of those players would go down in history not just as major-league superstars but as war heroes too.

Before the Japanese attack on Pearl Harbor, future Hall of Fame pitcher Bob Feller won seventy-six games for the Cleveland Indians in three seasons. The day after the attack, Feller enlisted in the US Navy. He was originally assigned to play baseball to entertain the troops, but he was eager to take on a more active role. After enrolling in gunnery school, he spent more than two years aboard the USS *Alabama*, serving heroically in the all-important Battle of the Philippine Sea and several other naval campaigns. When he returned to baseball after the war, Feller completed a career that included 279 complete games, forty-four shutouts, three no-hitters, and twelve one-hitters.

During the war, pitching great Bob Feller was the captain of a gun crew aboard one of America's battleships, and became one of the Navy's greatest heroes.

Warren Spahn pitched his first major league game for the Boston Braves in 1942, leaving to join the army later that same year. He spent the next three years fighting in some of the most heated land battles in the European theater including the pivotal Battle of the Bulge. After the war, he pitched in the major leagues into his forties. He won 363 games, pitched two no-hitters, and earned seventeen all-star selections, a Cy Young Award, and an induction into the Hall of Fame.

Boston Braves' star pitcher Warren Spahn fought in several key land battles and was also one of the military's great heroes.

Twenty-three-year-old Ted Williams, who was eventually to serve in two American wars, is shown here being sworn in to the nation's Naval Aviation Corps.

Ted Williams, famed for his above-.400 batting average in the 1941 season, served as a Marine Corps fighter pilot in World War II. Later, he would go on to fly thirty-nine missions in the Korean War where, on two occasions, his plane was damaged by ground fire. During that conflict, the man regarded as the greatest hitter of all time was awarded the Air Medal three times and the Presidential Medal of Freedom.

Catcher Yogi Berra was still in the minor leagues when he joined the US Navy. He became a gunner's mate and played a heroic role on D-Day. During the Allied invasion of Normandy, Berra piloted a rocket boat in front of the landing craft filled with troops, serving as a decoy to lure enemy fire away from the others. After the war, Berra spent another year in the minors before being called up to the Yankees where, in a twenty-three-year career, he won three Most Valuable Player Awards, played in fifteen all-star games, and contributed to thirteen Yankees' World Series wins before being inducted into the Hall of Fame.

Yogi Berra, destined to become a New York Yankee legend, was a hero of the largest military invasion in United States history: the Allied invasion of Normandy on June 6, 1944.

Two major leaguers, Elmer Gedeon, an outfielder with the Washington Senators, and Harry O'Neill, a catcher for the Philadelphia Athletics, made the ultimate sacrifice. Gedeon lost his life when his plane was shot down during a bombing raid on one of Germany's V-1 rocket-launching sites. O'Neill was killed during one of the fiercest campaigns in the war—the retaking of the Japanese-held island of Iwo Jima.

so, the Japanese attacked Pearl Harbor, America went to war, and all chances of moving came to an abrupt halt.

Over the next few seasons, however, in an unexpected way, the Browns found themselves with an on-field advantage. In the military draft system, men could be rejected from service because of ailments that would put them in danger when engaged in combat. Most of these ailments, however, did not impair their ability to play baseball. By some turn of fate, when in 1944 almost all the major league teams lost most of their prewar roster to the military, the Browns had eighteen ballplayers who remained with their team because they had been deemed unfit for duty—in official terms, they were classified "4-F."

Facing teams who had lost their stars to the war, the mostly intact 1944 Browns were finally on a level playing field with their opponents. They

In their quest for wartime players, the St. Louis Browns added one-armed Pete Gray to their roster.

ultimately wound up battling the Detroit Tigers for first place in the American League. Toward the end of the season, the Tigers superstar Dick Wakefield (who seemed on his way to winning the batting average, home run, and runs batted in crowns) was suddenly drafted, clearing the way for the Browns to claim the title. Still the Browns' pennant-winning record was 89-65, the lowest ever by an American League champion.

BASEBALL HAD GIVEN AMERICANS THE DISTRACTION THEY NEEDED, BECOMING MORE POPULAR THAN EVER IN THE PROCESS.

Unfortunately for the Browns, the 1944 pennant was their one and only great triumph. In the World Series against their crosstown rivals, the St. Louis Cardinals, they reverted to their old bumbling ways, batting just .189 as a team, striking out a third of the time they came to bat, and committing ten errors that led to seven Cardinal runs.

The absence of the true major leaguers had undeniably diminished the quality of play in both the American and National Leagues. But President Roosevelt had been right. Baseball had given Americans the distraction they needed, becoming more popular than ever in the process.

Enterprising Americans found ingenious new ways to keep baseball going during the war. Chicago Cubs owner Phillip Wrigley devised one of the most outlandish, newsworthy new ventures: a professional league based on the unlikely premise that women could play baseball, and play it well. And sure enough, the All-American Girls Professional Baseball League (AAGPBL) would boost national morale at a time when it needed it more than ever.

Wrigley began by sending thirty scouts throughout the United States and Canada searching for the best women baseball players they could find. Some 280 candidates were invited to Chicago's Wrigley Field for tryouts.

IMPRISONED

ON THE AMERICAN WEST COAST, where more than 120,000 Japanese Americans lived, Pearl Harbor had elicited the greatest emotions—and fears. To a person, these Americans of Japanese descent were loyal US citizens. But their worst fears were realized. The American government, concerned that some Japanese Americans might be spies or even saboteurs for their ancestral land, chose to take one of the most unjust and infamous actions in the nation's history. Although not a single case of spying or sabotage on the part of a Japanese American was ever discovered, the US government, with the aid of the military, placed 120,000 of its own citizens in barbed wire–enclosed internment camps for the long duration of the war.

For those interned, life in these camps, all of which were purposely located in the most inhospitable places, was extremely difficult in almost every way. But baseball had followed them to the camps. And for many, practically the only enjoyment they experienced during all their years of imprisonment was either watching or playing in the many games in the several leagues that internees established in the camps. George Omachi spoke for many of his fellow internees when, late in his life, he declared, "It was demeaning and humiliating to be incarcerated in your own country. Without baseball, camp life would have been miserable."

During World War II some 120,000 Japanese Americans (none of them ever proven anything but loyal American citizens) were placed in detention camps for the duration of the conflict. They found one of their few solaces playing and watching baseball games.

After putting them through rigorous drills, league officials selected what they regarded as the best sixty-four of them, and divided them into four teams—the Kenosha Comets and the Racine Belles in Wisconsin, the Rockford Peaches in Illinois, and the South Bend Blue Sox in Indiana. A 108-game schedule was arranged, and the three-month season was divided into two halves, with the winner of each half playing each other in a season-ending championship series.

The women of the AAGPBL came from almost every part of the country, but they all had one thing in common. "Pepper" Paire Davis, of the Racine Belles, explained it well: "We would rather play ball than eat."

For twelve years—far beyond the duration of the war that had prompted

Dorothy Kamenshek of the Rockford Peaches slides safely into third base.

Sophie Kurys, star base-stealer of the All-American Girls Professional Baseball Leagues' Racine Belles swipes yet another in her record number of thefts.

the league's creation—these women staked out space on the ballfield, quickly garnering monikers like "Queens of Swat" and "Belles of the Ball Game." As the league's longevity suggests, women's ball was more than just a subpar fill-in for the depleted men's league. As journalist Jack Fincher has written, "They weren't merely shadows of their male counterparts. They added dash and excitement to the national past time and, in so doing made it uniquely their own."

Every player in the league was highly talented, but Doris Sams may have been the best of them all. Playing in every season that the league was in operation, Sams performed exceptionally on the mound, in the outfield, and at the plate. She pitched both a perfect game and a no-hitter, and completed one season with 0.98 earned run average. She consistently hit above .300, won a batting crown and a home run title, and hit the longest home run in league history.

Dorothy Kamenshek of the Rockford Peaches was an equally remarkable player. "The finest first baseman I've ever seen, man or woman," was how former New York Yankees first baseman Wally Pipp described her. Kamenshek's teammate Rose Gacioch offered her own special praise, writing, "Kammie was ahead of her time. She used to make the split at first the way they do in the majors now. It's like they learned from her." During her ten-year AAGPBL career, Kamenshek was named to the league's all-star team a record seven times. She was the only player in the league's history to get over a thousand hits, finishing with an all-time record of 1,090. She had an amazing strikeout record of just one in every 46.12 times at bat. At the same time, she was a constant threat on the bases, finishing with 631 steals.

But the most unstoppable base stealer of all was the Racine Belles' Sophie Kurys, nicknamed Tina Cobb in homage to the legendary Ty Cobb. She set both the league and the world professional record by stealing 201 bases in just one season. Perhaps even more amazing, those 201 steals were accomplished in just 203 attempts. In her nine-year career, she racked up a total of 1,114 thefts, an average of almost 124 a season. Arguably the league's best all-around athlete, Kurys also excelled in basketball, track, volleyball, golf, and bowling.

Sams, Kamenshek, and Kurys were but three of the great superstars of

It did not take wartime baseball fans long to discover that the AAGPBL players were extremely talented ballplayers and that these games were filled with action.

the AAGPBL. There were many more, including slugger Audrey Wagner, who entered the league when she was only fifteen years old; Jean Faut, who pitched two perfect games, won Player of the Year honors twice, and finished her eight-year career with an earned run average of 1.23; and slick-fielding shortstop Dottie Schroeder, who the press labeled "the human vacuum cleaner" and of whom Chicago Cubs' manager Charlie Grimm said, "If she was a boy, I'd give $50,000 [$918,000 in today's money] for her."

As far as money was concerned, the salaries of between $800 and $1,500 a week in today's money that the AAGPBL players received placed them among the highest-paid women in the country. And, along with the satisfaction and the thrill they felt in being members of arguably the most advanced and successful female sports league ever established, almost to a player they were aware of the positive influence they were having throughout the country.

"The All-Americans were heroes for all their fans, but especially for their little girl fans," wrote Susan E. Johnson in her book *When Women Played Hardball*. "They showed us something difficult and dangerous, something that took physical courage, intelligence and a fighting spirit. Moreover, the ballplayers were doing this as a team, working hard with other women to achieve something worthwhile."

Deep in a South American jungle, U.S. soldiers cheer on the ballplayers back home during a radio broadcast.

The AAGPBL was a success, almost from the start. "At first," recalled Dottie Schroeder, "the fans came out of curiosity. But when they saw how good we were, they were hooked." So was the media. Radio stations, having successfully brought men's games to the airwaves, began broadcasting AAGPBL games. News shorts featuring clips from the league's games were continually

Within days of invading and taking control of the strategically placed Anzio territory in Italy, American troops were letting off steam by playing and watching baseball.

shown in movie theaters. Articles about the women and the league began appearing regularly in newspapers and magazines.

One magazine declared, "Not long ago, girl's baseball rated along with checkers for spectator interest. Now there are nights when you have to stand in the back to see what's going on at the plate." By the league's fifth year, one million fans were pouring into the ballparks.

"Some towns draw four times their population every season," stated one magazine. "If the New York Yankees stirred up that kind of excitement, they'd be drawing thirty-two million, instead of two million." By the late 1940s, the league had expanded to ten teams. A four-team minor league had been formed, junior leagues for girls as young as fourteen had been established, and players from the AAGPBL were making regular recruiting and exhibition tours across the United States, Cuba, and South America.

It seemed like it would go on forever, but it wasn't meant to be. By 1954,

WOMEN AT WAR

WORLD WAR II CHANGED THE UNITED STATES in an extraordinary number of ways. High on this list were the ways in which the conflict changed the nation for women and the ways in which women, in turn, transformed the nation.

When the war began, the vast majority of American women spent their days taking care of their homes and family. But with so many men overseas fighting the war, women were desperately needed to take on roles that had always been the exclusive domain of men.

And they did so in enormous numbers. More than six million women took wartime jobs in factories. Three million volunteered for the American Red Cross. Over 350,000 served in the military.

During World War II, the United States became the "arsenal of democracy," building not only the unprecedented amount of weapons and supplies needed by Americans but also by Great Britain and the United States' other allies. The millions of women factory workers worked long hours building airplanes, ships, trains, munitions, and countless other war products. They also worked in construction, drove trucks and streetcars, and performed clinical duties coast-to-coast.

In addition to the Army and Navy Nurse Corps, the more than 350,000 women who enlisted in the military served in one of the female corps established by each of the branches of the armed services—the WACs (Women's Army Corps), the WAVES (the US Navy's Women Accepted for Volunteer Duty), the Women Marines, the Coast Guards (SPARS), and the Army Air Forces' WASPs (Women Airforce Service Pilots). Among many other important tasks, these women in uniform repaired airplanes, operated radios, analyzed photographs, rigged parachutes, performed laboratory work, flew troop-transport planes, and served in units that delivered overseas mail. Although American

military policy prohibited females from engaging in combat, almost 550 women died in war-related incidents. Included among these casualties were sixteen nurses who were killed by enemy fire. More than 1,600 nurses were decorated for "bravery under fire and meritorious service."

World War II women defense-factory workers put the final touches on vital air force bomber parts.

things would change dramatically. A host of new stars would usher in a golden age for the men's major leagues. Television would take the nation by storm, with millions of people staying at home to watch major league men's games that were televised on a daily and nightly basis. As successful as the AAGPBL had become, it could not compete for fans with the expanding reach of the American and National Leagues. Though, ultimately, the women's league didn't last, it left an indelible mark on the women who played, on their fans, and on the game itself, buoying the nation through a pivotal moment in history.

While baseball was evolving on the home front, it was also cementing its place as "America's pastime" throughout the war-torn world. From the deserts of North Africa to the frozen tundra of Iceland, from the low countries of Holland and Belgium to the towering alpine nations, to places barely listed on the map, American troops, encouraged by their government, which built them ball fields around the globe, played baseball wherever they could. All told, more than 200,000 American servicemen played baseball across the European continent alone.

Even in England, a nation as devoted to cricket as Americans were to their national pastime, baseball, at least temporarily, took hold. Teams of American soldiers played games throughout Great Britain, often on diamonds hastily built upon soccer and rugby pitches, and attracted large crowds. British dignitaries, including Queen Mary, Mrs. Winston Churchill, and numbers of dukes, bishops, and local officials attended the games. Some even threw out the first ball. The American government's active support of baseball among the troops was evident in an inventory of equipment sent to England—86,964 baseball gloves, 72,850 baseballs, and 131,130 bats.

Baseball was equally prevalent in the Pacific theater. As the marines conquered island after island, the US Naval Construction Battalions, better known as the "Seabees," came in right behind them, building ball fields in such places as Guadalcanal, Saipan, Tarawa, and Guam. At the same time, US Army troops competed against one another in Australia, New Guinea,

The original caption to this photograph read: "These Yanks, forming an appreciative audience for a baseball game on the Anzio beachhead, could very easily be cheering a good hit, or riding the umpire for a slip-up in calling the balls. At any rate, they're happy, and if a simple baseball game can do this for them, let's have more of them!"

and the Philippines. As for the US Navy, every ship of any size had its own baseball team that faced off against marine or army teams whenever the ship arrived put into a port.

By spring of 1945, the war had turned decisively in the Allies' favor. And after Germany surrendered in May 1945, bringing the war in Europe to an end, baseball remained an essential element of the postwar operations. The high point of the US wartime baseball experience actually took place in September 1945, when two teams made up of the American occupying forces left in Europe to maintain order squared off in a best-of-five contest dubbed the GI World Series. One of these teams, the Germany division winners, was made up of major and minor league players representing the Seventy-First Division of the American Third Army. Its opponent was the best service team based in France and played under the cumbersome

Pupils at England's Harrod School are given a lesson in baseball by American airmen of the 225th Photo Recce Wing and the 305th Bomber Group.

name the Overseas Invasion Service Expedition (OISE) All-Stars.

Three of the games were to be played in an almost unimaginable site—the conquered German Stadion der Hitlerjugend (Stadium of the Hitler Youth) in Nuremberg, the infamous place where Adolf Hitler had held his massive Nazi Party rallies not long ago. The Seventy-First Division team, known as the Red Circlers (for the patch on their uniform shoulders), were heavy favorites. Led by major league superstars—namely, outfielder Harry "the Hat" Walker of the St. Louis Cardinals and star pitcher Ewell "the Whip" Blackwell of the Cincinnati Reds—the team also included major leaguers Johnny Wyrostek and Maurice Van Robays and several stars of the top minor leagues.

The French-based American team, the OISE All-Stars, was made up mostly of semiprofessional players. They did have one major league player, journeyman pitcher Sam Nahem, along with two other players who were stars of the Negro Leagues. Later, when the troops came home and baseball was at long last integrated, one of them, Willard Brown, would blast the first home run ever hit by a Black man in the American League. The other, Leon Day, a star pitcher for the Negro Leagues' Newark Eagles, would be regarded as too old to be brought up to the majors. The two of them would prove to be the stars of the heralded series.

More than 50,000 American service members, by far the largest baseball crowd in Europe during the war, poured into Nuremberg to witness the first game of the series. And it went as most expected. Ewell Blackwell baffled the OISE batters, striking out nine, while the OISE fielder committed seven errors, leading to a 9-2 Red Circlers victory.

The next afternoon, a crowd of more than 50,000 again made its way into the stadium. And they were treated to a thrilling comeback from OISE.

In this photograph, Japanese prisoners of war on the Pacific island of Guam engage in one of their favorite pastimes, playing ball.

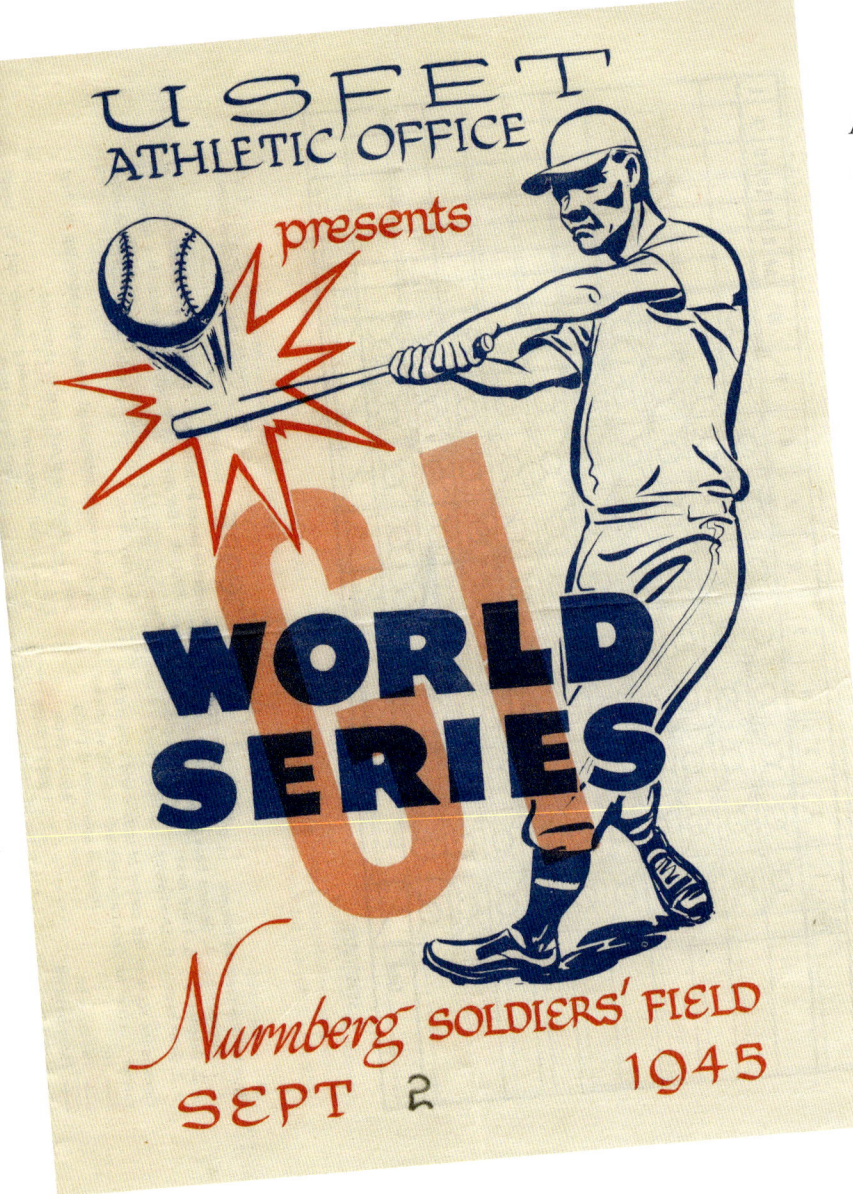

Program for the GI World Series in 1945 in Nuremberg, Germany.

Against the powerful Red Circlers lineup, Leon Day outdid Blackwell's first game performance by striking out ten and allowing only four hits. With a 2-1 victory the OISE had evened the series at one game apiece.

The following day, the two teams traveled to Rheims, France, to play the next two games at Headquarters Command Field. In game three, the OISE eked out another 2-1 win, putting themselves one game away from pulling off a colossal upset.

Order seemed to be restored the next day when, led by Harry Walker's two-run homer, the Red Circlers cruised to a 5-0 victory. It would all come down to the final game in Nuremberg.

And appropriately, the final game was as close as most of the series had been. As the American military newspaper, the *Stars and Stripes*, would later write, "The game was so close all the way through that it kept the crowd of over 50,000 on its feet cheering wildly and rewarding unfavorable decisions with sounds as wild as any ever to emerge from Ebbets Field or the Polo Grounds."

According to *The New York Times*, it was a deciding game "replete with miscues and thrills." In the seventh inning, with the Red Circlers ahead 1-0, Leon Day, who had been sent in to pinch-run, stole second base, and then stole third base, and came home on a fly ball to tie the game. The next inning, Willard Brown smashed a booming double to the deepest part of the ballpark, driving in what proved to be the winning run. The great upset had been achieved, fueled by Leon Day and Willard Brown. As journalist Robert Weintraub would later write, "What's striking about the games in Nuremberg is how little comment there was about the presence of the Negro League stars. If the throng on-hand knew what was coming just over the horizon, they might have paid more attention. They were witnessing an out-of-town preview of baseball's new frontier, a year and a half before [Jackie] Robinson's Brooklyn Dodgers debut."

Back in France, the victorious OISE team was honored with a huge parade and a steak and champagne dinner. "Day and Brown," observed one newspaper, "who would not be allowed to eat with their teammates in many major league towns, celebrated alongside their fellow soldiers."

Although the wartime years had changed both the nation and the game of baseball, it was fitting that America's pastime would be there to help embattled soldiers celebrate their hard-won victory in the European theater. Perhaps more surprising is the role that baseball played in the conflict on the other side of the globe, in the Pacific theater of World War II.

The OISE team photo.

JAPAN AND BASEBALL

IT WASN'T ALLIED SOLDIERS who brought baseball to Japan. By the time World War II was underway, the sport had long since woven its way into the fabric of Japanese culture. And although the war had pitted the United States and Japan against each other as mortal enemies, that animosity could not dampen Japan's affinity for "America's pastime." As in the United States, the war would irreversibly change baseball in Japan. And after the fighting was over, as the world was entering its next chapter, baseball would play a unique and crucial role in rebuilding the relationship between the two nations.

Baseball had been introduced to Japan by educator Horace Wilson, who, in 1872, was part of a wave of American high school and college instructors invited to Japan by a government anxious to Westernize, in a country long anchored around ancient traditions and self-imposed isolation from the rest of the world. Neither Wilson nor his colleagues could have imagined how quickly and how completely the Japanese would fall in love with the game. As one Japanese writer put it, "Baseball

From the time baseball was introduced into their nation, the Japanese discovered great joy in yakyu.

From the beginning, baseball in Japan drew huge crowds. This crowd had gathered for a game played at recreation grounds in Kobe, Japan.

is perfect for us. If the Americans hadn't invented it, we probably would have."

By the 1890s, baseball had grown so popular in Japan's high schools and colleges that it had essentially become the country's national sport. And in the early 1900s, an initiative known as the "goodwill tours" strengthened baseball's hold on Japan even further. They began with American and Japanese college teams crossing the Pacific to play each other. These games drew huge crowds and inspired further visits. Soon, players from the American minor leagues were organizing their own tours to Japan. The mostly female Philadelphia Bobbies and the Negro Leagues' Philadelphia Royal Giants also made trips to Japanese stadiums in the early years of the 1900s.

Its embrace of transcontinental baseball games was one of many ways

Japan relaxed its isolationist policies during this era. Inspired by Western nations, Japan industrialized its economic system to gain manufacturing power, linked the country with railroads and telegraph lines, and strengthened its military. Despite the challenges posed by its status as an island nation—especially, the limited natural resources available on the island—the country developed rapidly into a sophisticated world leader.

Meantime, there were youngsters playing baseball in every section of Japan.

By the 1930s, the game had become so popular it was claimed there were more youngsters playing baseball in Japan than in the United States. And amazingly, in an era without television, most of these youngsters knew the names of great American ballplayers and regarded them as heroes. These fans were eager for the opportunity to see top stars of the American diamond in action.

In 1931, many of them got their wish when a team of American major leaguers including Lou Gehrig, Lefty Grove, Mickey Cochrane, and Al Simmons traveled to Japan for a series of seventeen games.

"I have seen some excited crowds in baseball," Lou Gehrig told a sportswriter after the first game on tour, "but nothing before like this. I do not know of anything in my entire career that has touched me as much as this welcome. It seemed like something out of a dream. It will be difficult to try to give a description of it to

The all-female Philadelphia Bobbies were one of the many American teams that toured Japan.

The earliest organized Japanese baseball began in the universities. Here we see the 1916 Waseda University team.

any of the fans and ballplayers in America. They will all think you are exaggerating."

In the seventeen games, the American all-stars drew more fans than the Pittsburgh Pirates had attracted back home all year in seventy-seven contests. People traveled hundreds of miles and lined up at dawn for the chance to buy tickets. The tour drew almost 500,000 people, caused a huge sensation in the Japanese press, and earned millions in today's dollars.

The original caption to this photograph read: "It is next to blasphemy to hit over unblessed ball grounds and so these Shinto priests are going through their prayer ceremonies on the opening day of the baseball season."

But despite its huge success and the enormous attention it drew, as far as the Japanese fans were concerned, there was one big thing lacking in the 1931 tour: Babe Ruth. To people around the world, Babe Ruth *was* baseball. He had changed the game with his monster home runs and clutch performances. The only thing bigger than his batting average and home run totals was his personality.

In the 1930s, there was only one person who could persuade Ruth to leave the comforts of home in the offseason and embark on a tour of Japan. It was Lefty O'Doul, a former teammate of the Babe's, the manager of the Pacific Coast League's San Francisco Seals, and the greatest promoter of Japanese baseball in America. Using their friendship and all his considerable persuasive skills, O'Doul convinced Ruth to take part in the next Japanese tour of American major leaguers, scheduled for 1934.

Led by Ruth, with five other future Hall of Famers on the squad, the 1934 tour managed to surpass even

Legendary American first baseman Lou Gehrig blasted a home run during this well-attended contest between a major league All-Star team and a team from Japan.

JAPAN AND BASEBALL ♦ 143

LEFTY O'DOUL

Before he became known as the "Father of Japanese Baseball," Lefty O'Doul was an acclaimed major league ballplayer and an equally successful minor league manager. During his seven years in the major leagues, O'Doul won two batting titles, while compiling a career batting average of .349. As manager of the Pacific Coast League's San Francisco Seals, he not only won several championships but also proved himself to be one of the best teachers of the sport.

O'Doul was also arguably the greatest spokesperson for the game of baseball, which made him a natural selection to lead the "goodwill tours" to Japan every year from 1933 to 1937 that had such a profound effect on both countries. But O'Doul's involvement with baseball in the country that, for so many centuries, had been closed to the outside world did not end there. Toward the end of the series of tours, O'Doul had become alarmed at the growing militarism he observed in Japan. And the attack on Pearl Harbor devastated him. But his warm feelings for the Japanese people remained, and after the war the United States government would turn to O'Doul to use baseball to help relieve the bitter feelings that came out of the conflict.

Throughout the 1950s, O'Doul continued to bring Major League Baseball (MLB) star players to Japan, including Joe and Dom DiMaggio and Yogi Berra. He also arranged for Japanese ballplayers to participate in American spring training. And in 1953, he achieved one of his biggest goals when he brought the New York Giants across the Pacific, the first entire MLB team to travel to Japan. In 2002, Lefty O'Doul became the first American elected to the Japanese Baseball Hall of Fame.

All-star player and manager Lefty O'Doul was a driving force in bringing baseball to the great heights it reached in Japan.

the triumphs of the 1931 visit. About 100,000 people were on hand to greet the All-Americans when they arrived in Yokohama. That was nothing compared to the Ruth-led heroes' arrival in Tokyo, where between a half million and one million fans turned out to see the superstars.

Enthralled Japanese baseball fans bellowed, "Banzai, Babe Ruth!" as a motorcade rolled through the city, a beaming Ruth riding atop a convertible, drinking in the adulation and yelling "Banzai!" (May you live 10,000 years!) right back. Almost 60,000 spectators crammed into Jingu Stadium for the first game in Tokyo. All told, the tour's eighteen contests drew three quarters of a million people. The Babe's performance (he played every inning) can only be described as Ruthian. He hit .408 during the tour and led his team in runs batted in and home runs as well.

Babe Ruth was one of the best-known individuals in the world. Here he signs a baseball for the prince and princess of Japan.

Some of the greatest crowds ever seen in Japan were those who turned out to cheer the great Babe Ruth when he arrived for one of his tours.

Clowning with the kids he encountered throughout Japan, posing for pictures wherever he went, and, most important, blasting thirteen home runs in eighteen games, Babe Ruth became almost as big a hero in Japan as he was in America. The tour offered a stark contrast with the diplomatic tensions already beginning to develop between the two countries, over America's refusal to sell Japan oil and other products it desperately needed and the United States' growing alarm over the number of warships Japan was adding to its fleet. "Diplomats and admirals," stated the *Chicago Tribune*, "are arguing over oil and navies, but the Japanese populace found a common ground of agreement today with Americans—baseball and Babe Ruth."

As with all the tours of American players to Japan, the ranks of the Japanese teams they played against were filled with highly talented stars of the Japanese high school leagues. And, as far as the Japanese fans were concerned, Babe Ruth was not the only hero of the 1934 tour. There was another shining star worthy of celebration—and he was one of their own. His name was Eiji Sawamura, and, although only seventeen, he was already well known in Japanese baseball, considered to be the best pitcher in the talent-filled high school leagues. On a sun-drenched afternoon in jam-packed Kusanagi Stadium, he had the chance to face off against some of the greatest baseball players in the world.

In the first inning, seventeen-year-old Sawamura played admirably, even striking out future Hall of Famer Charlie Geringher. But in the second inning, he faced the heart of the American all-stars' lineup—a true murderers' row. First up was Babe Ruth himself. And Sawamura struck him out on three pitches. Next to the plate was Lou Gehrig. As the Japanese crowd roared in delight, the teenager struck him out too. Finally, Jimmie Foxx, one of the greatest sluggers ever to play the game, stepped into the box. And with the noise in the stadium absolutely deafening, Sawamura fanned him as well. The high schooler had made quick work of four Hall of Famers in a row.

Eli Sawamura was one of the greatest and most admired players in all of Japanese baseball history.

Sawamura went on to pitch the rest of the game against the superstars, losing 1-0 on his one mistake, a home run ball to Lou Gehrig, but becoming a national hero in the process. Newspapers across the country played up the close game in nationalistic terms, suggesting that one day there would be a Japanese–United States World Series and that Japan would have an excellent chance of beating the Americans.

But before a transnational World Series could become a reality, Japan would need an organized professional

Everyone loved Babe Ruth, none more than kids, and the affection transcended oceans and national boundaries.

league of its own. Luckily, almost as soon as the 1934 tour ended, Japanese newspaper magnate Matsutaro Shoriki began making good on his promise to start the country's first professional league. He recruited many of the players who had faced the Americans during the tour, forming a team that would eventually become the Tokyo Giants, by far the most successful franchise in Japanese professional baseball, then and now. Unsurprisingly, during its earliest years, Eiji Sawamura was its ace pitcher.

By 1941, Japanese professional teams were well established and thriving, but the political climate was shifting rapidly. Japan's most militant leaders had gained control of the government, and Japanese forces had captured China's capital and much of the Pacific world. In retaliation, the United States had cut off all shipments of fuel, steel, and scrap iron—products that Japan had long relied upon getting from America.

With the December 7, 1941, attack on Pearl Harbor, the United States and Japan became mortal enemies. A few days after the surprise assault, baseball's newspaper the *Sporting News*—which in 1934 had declared "we are all brothers"—now exclaimed, "[Japan] may have acquired a little skill at the game, but the soul of our National Game never touched them."

Americans could disavow Japanese baseball, but they couldn't stop their enemy from playing the game. And surprisingly, considering the game's American origins, Japan came to the same decision that Roosevelt and Kenesaw Landis had about the sport's fate during the war: baseball should go on.

Yes, the Japanese professional teams kept playing ball— but many of the nation's leaders pushed to sever the game's associations with the United States. All Western baseball terminology was banned from the game. The Tokyo Giants, who had been named by Lefty O'Doul, became the Kyojin-gun. The teams' uniforms, long modeled after those worn by American teams, were replaced by khakis and military hats. And in order to project a military spirit, tie games were also banned under the rationale that all conflicts including those in baseball should be "fought to the bitter end."

Like in the United States, many players in the Japanese Professional League were called upon to serve their country. Some seventy-two of them would die fighting for Japan, eleven of them in 1941 alone. Among them was Shinichi Ishimaru who, in his second and third years in the league, pitched for Nagoya and won a total of thirty-seven games. After the 1943 season, he joined the Japanese Navy and became a kamikaze pilot—his assignment was to sacrifice his life by diving his airplane directly into an American warship in an attempt to sink the vessel.

Ishimaru's suicide mission took place on May 11, 1945. He made his way to his plane, carrying with him a baseball and a glove. Turning to one of his fellow pilots, he told him, "I'll get in the plane after I throw ten strikes." After the tenth strike, he lay down his glove, tied a headband with the word "Courage" around his head, and climbed into the cockpit. He was shot down by the Americans well before he reached his target, a warship operating in the Sea of Japan.

"I'LL GET IN THE PLANE AFTER I THROW TEN STRIKES."

Another well-known victim of the war was Masaki Yoshihara, who had been Eiji Sawamura's catcher during all his great victories. A favorite of the Tokyo Giants fans, Yoshihara was hailed as a "stubborn and fierce competitor, the best-ever Giants catcher, always full of vigor leading his teammates with a loud raucous voice."

In 1941, after leading the Giants to the league title, Yoshihara was

Star Japanese Leagues pitcher Shinichi Ishimaru was one of countless numbers of Japanese professional ballplayers to die in combat in World War II.

drafted into the Japanese army. In an interview with the leading sports magazine, *Yakyakai*, Yoshihara told his fans, "Now with a fond memory I am going to leave the dear baseball world to which I fiercely devoted my youthful ardor." He never returned, succumbing to disease while serving in Burma in 1944. He was twenty-five years old.

As for Eiji Sawamura, the future was similarly clouded. In 1936, the former high school superstar, the young man who had attained legendary status by striking out Charlie Gehringer, Babe Ruth, Lou Gehrig, and Jimmie Fox in succession, had pitched the Japanese Baseball League's first no-hitter. The next year he won the Triple Crown of pitching—games won, earned runs average, and strikeouts. Then, in 1938, as Japan continued to attack China, he was drafted into the army. There, not surprisingly, he immediately exhibited a great skill at throwing grenades. He tossed so many grenades, in fact, that he damaged his pitching arm.

Returning to civilian life and the Professional Baseball League, Sawamura was not the same pitcher he had been. He pitched until 1943 when he announced his retirement. In 1944, he was drafted again, and on December 2, his troop ship was making its way toward the combat zone when it was

150 ♦ BASEBALL'S SHINING SEASON

sunk by an American submarine, the USS Sea Devil, and, along with most everyone else aboard, the still-young man, who had been one of the world's most celebrated baseball players, lost his life.

In 1945, the United States finally brought World War II to a definitive end with nuclear blasts at Hiroshima and Nagasaki. Elation at the monumental new advantage the United States now possessed, and awe at the power of the bomb, soon mingled with deep, unsettling contemplation of what it meant to live in a world where humanity had the means to destroy itself. For the moment, though, the fact was that the United States had the unanswerable ability to defeat any foe immediately. The blast had spared the estimated 200,000 American lives a ground invasion of Japan would have cost. And the United States could dictate the terms of peace to Japan, which it did.

Relations between the United States and Japan could not have been at a lower point. But in the years that followed, baseball would play a major role in bringing the two nations back together.

General Douglas MacArthur, commander of the American occupation forces in Japan, a man who had played baseball at West Point, recognized the

U.S. Marines vs. Japanese team in Saga City, Japan.

When American-Japanese relations were restored after World War II, American player tours of Japan resumed. Here, Joe DiMaggio demonstrates batting techniques to young Japanese ballplayers.

potential that baseball had for healing even the most serious rifts. He and the other authorities in charge of the postwar occupation of Japan were certain that baseball could also help the ruined Japanese nation turn the corner to starting anew.

On November 18, 1945, in the same stadium where Babe Ruth had thrilled enormous crowds just a few years earlier, a team of Japanese ballplayers took the field against a team of occupying American soldiers. "Spectators [numbering] 45,000 would not leave the stadium even after the game was over and the evening was drawing in," recalled the game's organizer Yoichi Aida. Before 1945 was over, the Japanese Baseball League, now called the Nippon Professional Baseball League, had resumed operations and was getting ready for a full 1946 season.

In 1949, with World War II now having been over for four years and with American troops still occupying Japan, General Douglas MacArthur, sensing an opportunity to help rebuild relations between the two countries, asked Lefty O'Doul to organize another goodwill tour. Although it had been more than twelve years since O'Doul had brought American ballplayers to Japan, and although he had been both devastated and outraged at Japan's assault on Pearl Harbor, O'Doul responded enthusiastically to MacArthur's request and brought his entire San Francisco Seals team across the Pacific to play a ten-game series against the Tokyo Giants.

From the moment O'Doul and his team arrived in Tokyo, it was clear that the tour was going to be an enormous success. More than a million people greeted the Seals on the streets of Tokyo. Almost 100,000 spectators attended some of the games. For the Japanese, it was an enormous boost for the sport they had never stopped loving—and a reminder of what the two nations had in common. There was still much work to do to repair the country and its relationship with the United States, but the game of baseball had provided hope that it could be done.

American Major League touring teams consistently drew enormous numbers of fans to Japanese stadiums. Lefty O'Doul drives in a run before a crowd of more than 50,000 spectators.

JAPANESE STARS
OF AMERICAN BASEBALL

IN 2021, SHOHEI OHTANI became the MLB's first full-time two-way player since Babe Ruth more than a hundred years earlier. In games when he did not play a regular position, he was a starting pitcher—a testament to his once-in-a-century level of talent. He won the American League's Most Valuable Player Award after having one of the greatest individual seasons in baseball history. At the plate, he hit forty-six home runs, and on the mound, he compiled a 3.18 earned run average. Thanks to his exceptional performance, he became the first player in MLB history to be selected to the all-star game both as a hitter and a pitcher. In 2024, Ohtani became the first major leaguer ever to hit fifty home runs (fifty-four) and steal more than fifty bases (fifty-nine) in a single season. As a result, Ohtani was the unanimous winner of the 2024 National League Most Valuable Player award. Born in Oshu, Iwate, Japan, and a product of Japanese major leagues, Ohtani is the latest in a line of Japanese players who have strengthened the link between American and Japanese baseball by becoming stars in the United States.

Third and fourth from left: Hideki Matsui and Shohei Ohtani.

The first Japanese ballplayer to play in the American major leagues was left-handed pitcher Masanori Murakami who, in 1965, after a brief debut a year earlier, made eighty-five appearances for the San Francisco Giants. He was one of the top strikeout pitchers in the National League before, for personal reasons, returning to Japan.

The ballplayer credited with truly paving the way into the American major leagues for fellow Japanese players was Hideo Nomo, who began his career with the Los Angeles Dodgers in 1995 by winning the National League's Rookie of the Year

Masanori Murakami (left) shakes hands with Tsuyoshi Wada.

Hideo Nomo

Award. In a sparkling twelve-year career, Nomo won 123 games, pitched two no-hitters, and twice led the league in strikeouts.

Among the other Japanese stars of the major leagues are as follows:

ICHIRO SUZUKI

One of the most outstanding players in American major league history thus far, the ballplayer known simply as Ichiro began his twelve-year career with the Seattle Mariners in 2001. In his extraordinary rookie season, he led the American League in hits with 242, in batting average (.350), and steals (56). This unprecedented accomplishment earned him the league's Most Valuable Player Award, the Rookie of the Year Award, and the Silver Slugger and Golden Glove Awards. Before his career was over, Ichiro would go on to earn ten consecutive all-star game selections, ten consecutive Golden Glove Awards, three Silver Slugger Awards, and two batting titles. In 2004, he set the single-season hits record with 262.

Ichiro Suzuki

HIDEKI MATSUI

During a ten-year career, mostly with the Yankees, Matsui hit 175 home runs and drove in 760 runs. Twice an American League all-star, he was the 2009 World Series most valuable player and remains the only Japanese-born player to win that award.

YU DARVISH

One of the greatest pitchers in Nippon Professional Baseball history, Yu Darvish joined the Texas Rangers in 2012. He then went on to pitch for the Los Angeles Dodgers, Chicago Cubs, and San Diego Padres. Darvish has the distinction of being runner-up for the Cy Young Award (given to the season's best pitcher) in both the American and the National Leagues. He also reached the thousand-strikeout mark faster than anyone in MLB history (812 innings).

8
THE FUTURE BEGINS

In a scene repeated again and again once World War II ended, 4,000 American servicemen arrive home after having seen combat in Europe.

IN THE FOUR YEARS THAT AMERICA was fighting World War II, the country transformed. When the fighting finally concluded in 1945, the nation, and baseball, would be markedly different from what players and fans had left behind in 1941.

During the war, millions of Americans relocated. More than seven million men and women went overseas, and others were sent to military bases far from home. Millions more moved to take jobs in war factories and supply houses as the nation expanded its already enormous economic capacity. Urban city centers boomed, and so did the South and West, where many military bases were located.

To move troops and supplies to military bases over the first half of the 1940s, the federal government had helped states build better roads, and started planning for a national network of superhighways for national defense and economic development. In the second part of the decade, road improvements started making it easier for people to leave their longtime homes and seek better lives, adding to a population boom in

President Franklin D. Roosevelt signs the "G.I. Bill of Rights," which provided broad benefits for veterans of World War II.

the South and West and setting the stage for the growth of suburbs in the coming years.

The return of millions of soldiers, sailors, and other servicemen and women in 1945 and 1946 did not prompt a return to the old pattern of living. It only fanned the fires of transformation.

Operation Magic Carpet, the return of almost eight million Americans from fifty-five different areas of combat around the world in less than a year, according to the National WWII Museum, was "the largest combined air and sealift ever organized." An average of 22,000 veterans returned home every single day for a year.

All those returning veterans needed jobs, and so did most of the people who'd served at home. With the Great Depression close in the nation's collective memory, economic planners knew that fifteen million people leaving the military, all looking for work at the same time, was a recipe for a second economic collapse. So in 1944, Congress passed legislation known as the GI Bill—laws that provided, among other benefits, low-interest loans to World War II veterans so they could buy homes, and free tuition so they could go back to college, keeping them from returning to the workforce all at once.

The most immediate impact of this historic legislation was that people started pouring out of the cities and into the suburbs via freshly paved highways. In just a few years (1946–1950), farming towns were transformed from sleepy rural locales to busy "bedroom communities" where homeowners commuted to and from their jobs on increasingly crowded roads.

This historic population shift was not without consequence, of course.

The privilege of moving to the suburbs was reserved, as were many privileges, for white families. Average income and quality of life in the older cities declined. That lowered property tax payments from homeowners, and municipal service eroded. A vicious cycle resulted, and in a few decades many families of color found themselves trapped in unappealing city cores with poor schools, while white families advanced. Postwar prosperity benefited nearly all Americans, but it benefited white Americans more. A great migration of Black citizens fleeing excruciating discrimination in the South accelerated the new ethnic schism between city and suburb.

All this investment—in housing, education, transportation, the retooling of factories to make civilian goods—led to a revolution in the American way of life, and the largest economic boom the world had ever seen. Americans invented the phrase "consumer culture," and lived it out.

What was seen by some as "screwball materialism," as journalist Lance Morrow put it, was seen by many more as simply a fulfillment of the American dream—a house (full of brightly colored gadgets and appliances), a car,

An aerial view of Levittown, New York, built to help meet the need for housing for returning servicemen and their families after World War II.

In the seasons following World War II more and more major league ballgames were played under the lights.

and a nice yard in the suburbs. This vision of the perfect life was sold hard by the nation's burgeoning marketing industry, and millions of people bought it—if they could. Discrimination in home sales, loan approval, and employment opportunities meant that this suburban American dream was largely for whites only.

Through all this, the nation welcomed baseball home as if it were a GI coming home from the warfront. Attendance at games soared, and the sport's reach expanded alongside the nation's migration patterns. Big-league baseball teams (white men–only major league ball, that is) had never been located west of the Mississippi or south of Atlanta, but after the postwar migration, that would not be the case for long. The game continued to grow internationally too. By 1946, high-quality pro ball was firmly established in Japan, although the notion of Japanese players appearing in the American major leagues was still two decades away. At the same time, the number of players and leagues in Latin America exploded. The big leagues took note, increasing scouting for talent overseas, foretelling in particular a major influx of Latino players in coming decades.

> ...NIGHT GAMES SUITED THE FANS, AND THEREFORE WOULD BE AN INEVITABLE PART OF THE FUTURE.

Back home, the game took on new life. Teams celebrated the return of their stars from combat, happy to be at full strength once again. To many war veterans, baseball seemed like an appealing career path, especially "after a hitch in the army," and on the front page of the *Sporting News* on March 28, 1946, reports from training camp noted a distinct uptick in injuries—likely the result of new big-league hopefuls who hadn't been quite prepared for what would be required of them to make the cut.

That same front page had a story about the increasing number of night games. Yankee Stadium, which had never had lights before, planned fourteen night contests in 1946, and there were a record 258 night games on the schedule league wide. The players didn't like it, and neither did baseball writers, the *Sporting News* reported, but night games suited the fans, and therefore would be an inevitable part of the future.

Integration, television, movement westward—America would undergo profound changes in the 1940s, and other exciting things were still to come. Baseball would try to keep pace, and its fans would come to see that 1941 had been the end of an era for both the country and the sport.

Technology of all kinds transformed life in rural areas and cities alike. When the decade opened, horses still pulled plows in the country and it wasn't unheard of for city dwellers to use iceboxes to keep food cool—relying on heavy ice blocks delivered by horse carriage. A sizeable portion of rural America lived without electric power and indoor plumbing; the telephone

THE INVENTION OF THE TEENAGER

The end of World War II brought with it a host of new inventions. Of all of them, certainly the most unusual, and arguably most important, was the invention of the "teenager." People had been turning thirteen for millions of years, but not until the postwar years did this become regarded as a special thing, something that deserved its own name. Three factors can be credited with creating the teenager and teenage culture. They were the rise of the high school, which gave youngsters between thirteen and eighteen a place to build a separate culture away from their family; the booming marketing industry, which identified teenagers as a lucrative demographic on which to focus; and the automobile, which gave teens a new level of independence.

Following the war, teenagers in convertible automobiles became a common sight on streets and roads throughout America.

Of the three, the automobile may have been the most notable. During World War II, almost no cars were manufactured. But as soon as the conflict ended, they poured off the assembly lines in record numbers. And because the automobile dramatically shrunk distance, teenagers' universes were expanded, affecting dating, friendship, recreation, education, and work.

The automobile was intertwined with another major factor instrumental in the building of teenage culture: consolidated high school. In previous generations, tens of thousands of teenaged youngsters had been part of the nation's labor pool. After child labor was banned in the United States in 1938, they became students. Just as buses and automobiles made it easier for a huge number of people to get to major league ballparks, they transported students to schools (often far from their homes), throwing more teenagers together than ever before. At the same time, states throughout the country passed laws extending the school day and the school year. As teenagers spent more time together, they developed their own customs and ways of life. "The abolition of child labor and the lengthening span of formal education," stated *The New York Times*, "have given us a huge leisure class of the young with animal energies."

Marketers quickly realized that this brand-new category of people, now officially called teenagers, offered an enormous market opportunity with, thanks to their parents, enormous spending power. And teenagers had their own tastes that could set trends and shape culture. As the History Channel's Allison McNearney has written, "this was the age of getting cozy at the drive-ins and cruising around town. It was during this time that a new form of music was born, one that would become the anthem of teenagers around the world. It was called rock and roll."

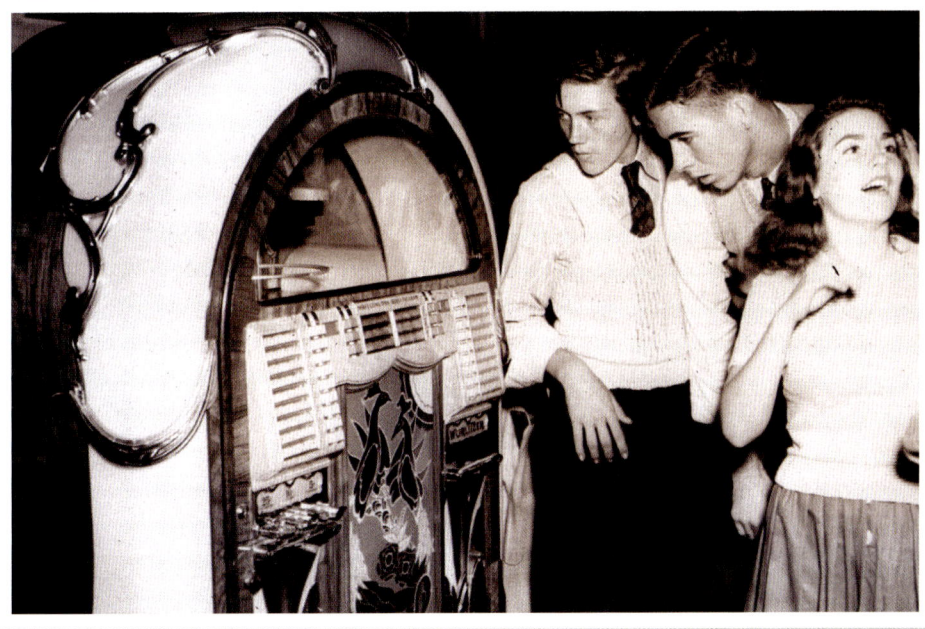

In the early postwar years, jukeboxes provided much of the music to which teens danced and listened.

UNION DIME SAVINGS BANK
Entrance —— Second Door to Right ——▶

was considered a luxury by working-class families in the cities. By 1950, cars and lights and running water and electric appliances were overwhelmingly the norm.

The war had spurred development of all kinds of new technology, from computers to plastics, and nearly all of them, unknown in 1941, eventually made an impact on the game of baseball. The jet plane made coast-to-coast games manageable, radar technology allowed scouts to measure pitch speed, and computers eventually would radically alter the way teams, batters, pitchers, and managers analyzed the game and played it.

The technology with perhaps the biggest and most immediately visible impact on baseball in the 1940s was none other than the television.

Television had been developing since the 1930s, and sure enough, one of the first events broadcast outside the studio was a ball game between Columbia and Princeton in 1939. By 1941, television, with seven thousand sets in use (almost all in and around New York City), began to attract advertisers, and the first TV commercial in history aired July 1, 1941—during a baseball game. It was a ten-second spot for Bulova watches. By 1950, the number of sets in America had grown from seven thousand to four million. National surveys showed that television was now the country's most popular form of entertainment. Baseball executives, initially resistant to broadcasting the games on radio, embraced the

Television dramatically changed the way millions of people experienced baseball. Here, in a scene common before most Americans had television in their homes, a crowd gathers to watch a game made available to them on a television set in a department store window.

THE FUTURE BEGINS ◆ 165

For more than a century baseball had been the unchallenged national pastime. In the years following the war, pro football became increasingly popular.

televising of them from the beginning. Most were convinced, rightly so it turned out, that the live action TV captured so vividly would lure people into the ballparks.

Television also offered Americans a multitude of other entertainment options that competed with baseball for their attention. Ultimately, the invention would make football the country's most popular sport by the 1970s. Along with basketball, which also soared in interest, football was easier to capture than baseball on TV cameras, and the quick action and fixed time limits of football were better paced for an America in a hurry. And because professional football games aired once a week for about sixteen weeks rather than 154 times a year, each televised game was a highly anticipated, novel event.

Little by little, baseball gained a reputation as a game for an earlier, slower era. Although it never fully shook off its moniker as "America's pastime," by the late 1940s, baseball's days as the nation's most popular sport were numbered.

Alongside the country's technological progress, the 1940s also ushered in vast social movements that would shape the future. The war had postponed a reckoning over worker rights and civil rights that burst to prominence in peacetime. Hundreds of labor unions held strikes in 1946 and 1947, including a railroad strike that paralyzed the nation (and underscored how trains, not trucks, were still the primary way America moved its cargo).

Baseball was not immune from this unrest. The summer of 1946 brought the first serious attempt to unionize ballplayers, with the Pittsburgh Pirates as the test case, demanding a minimum $7,500 salary and better worker rights. The players voted 20-16 in favor of a strike on June 7—but that was just under the two-thirds support required to move forward, and the union failed. When the Pirates took the field, fans in the heavily unionized Steel City booed their own team.

The unionization of ballplayers would not come until 1966, but the 1946 season would be notable for another milestone in the area of civil rights—and as the game made progress, it brought the nation forward with it.

More than one and a half million African Americans served in the US military forces during World War II. They fought in the Pacific, Mediterranean, and European war zones, including the pivotal Battle of the Bulge and the invasion of Normandy. But even as it proclaimed itself the exemplar of freedom for the world to emulate, America lived out a very different reality, on the field and off. The Black soldiers who returned having supposedly protected such principles as "all men are created equal" were told to go back to segregated communities where, in the South, their children could not study with white neighbors. And Black ballplayers may have served their nation proudly—in segregated units—but they were still barred from playing in the major leagues.

> **AMERICA LIVED OUT A VERY DIFFERENT REALITY, ON THE FIELD AND OFF.**

However, as more and more white people began questioning, and in many cases, became ashamed of this reality, this hypocrisy would not be tolerated for much longer.

The 1946 major league season, like all the others since the 1880s, was for white players only. But it was the last segregated season. As early as 1942, Branch Rickey, owner of the Brooklyn Dodgers, had begun laying plans to bring a Black ballplayer up through the Dodgers system and into the majors.

BABY BOOMERS

In the early 1900s, due to several factors, the United States experienced a gradual but steady decline in its birth rate. These factors included a widespread move from the farm to the city where large families were a greater burden to support. Later in the 1900s, during the Great Depression, when money was scarcer than it had ever been, the nation's birth rate fell to its lowest point ever.

Following World War II, however, the United States experienced an unprecedented rise in its birth rate, commonly referred to as "the baby boom." Between 1946 and 1964, an average of 4.24 million new babies were born every year.

There were several reasons for this historic development. High among them was the fact that millions of soldiers, sailors, marines, and airmen, weary of the stress and dangers of war, were anxious to settle down to normal family life. And they had this desire during a postwar period of unprecedented economic growth, a time when there was widespread optimism that this would last, a time when, thanks to an act of Congress known as the GI Bill, the promise of access to a good job and affordable housing, which was available to most veterans of the war, made raising a family particularly desirable.

The baby boomers grew up during a period of economic and population growth, years that saw great advances in areas such as medicine, years of huge industrial expansion. Most significantly, they were raised and came to maturity in an era of enormously significant political events. All of which led them as a whole to be characterized by restlessness, a propensity for hard work, and a strong desire for social change.

The baby boomers had a huge influence on almost every aspect of American culture. This was particularly true in the 1960s and 1970s when constituting as much as 40 percent of the American population, the "boomers" were at the forefront of social change including the civil rights movement, the protests against the Vietnam War, and the feminist movement.

It would give his club a competitive advantage on the field, to be sure, but Rickey also could see the growing anti-segregation movement around him, and agreed with it. But he also knew he would need to find just the right player to cross the color line—one who had not just superb baseball ability, but also the temperament to endure the storm of abuse he was sure to get from white players and fans alike.

Rickey found his player in Jackie Robinson of Pasadena, California, a phenomenal athlete who was just developing his baseball skills in the Negro Leagues. In a now-famous meeting in the summer of 1945, Rickey asked Robinson if he could take all the taunts and rough play that certainly would

In an event that would change both baseball and America forever, Jackie Robinson became the first African American to sign a contract with a major league team or its affiliate.

Youngsters, anxious to get Jackie Robinson's autograph, reach into the Dodgers' dugout.

come. "Are you looking for a Negro who is afraid to fight back?" Robinson recalled asking Rickey. The owner replied, "I'm looking for a Negro with enough guts not to fight back." Robinson agreed to be the one, and Rickey signed him.

The story of Robinson's first year in the big leagues, the discrimination he faced (for example, he could not stay at the team motel in the South during spring training), the mistreatment he endured—and the way he helped lift baseball to a higher level—has become one of the most legendary and most inspiring in American history. Within months of Robinson's signing, baseball started integrating for real. By the end of the 1950 season, twelve Black ballplayers were playing in the major leagues. Many, many more were about to follow, and the Negro Leagues, increasingly depleted of stars, diminished in quality and importance and ceased to operate by 1960.

Jackie Robinson joined the major leagues in 1947. In 1948, President

Harry S. Truman outlawed discrimination in federal hiring, and desegregated the military. Integration on the baseball diamond had proved to be an important catalyst for larger improvements across the nation for Black Americans, which would continue through to the civil rights movement in the decades to come. Although full equality would continue to elude us even to this day, the abolishment of baseball's color line was an unmistakable sign of progress.

Meanwhile, the changes in the ways Americans lived continued to accelerate. By 1950, there were six million television sets in the nation and the percentage of American homes with telephones had risen from 37 percent in 1941 to 62 percent. Long-distance phone service and soon jet travel shrunk distances as never before. Cars and roads had become better than ever before. Fast food was invented.

With travel becoming easier and easier, Black people streamed into northern cities, while white people poured out of the cities and moved into the South and West in record numbers. And by 1953, baseball was ready to catch up with the changing nation. The Braves moved out of Boston and

This aerial view shows the new Dodger stadium on its opening day as 56,000 spectators cheered on the Dodgers and the Cincinnati Reds. The movement of the Dodgers and the Giants to the West Coast made major league baseball truly a national pastime.

WORLD WAR II INVENTIONS
THAT CHANGED THE WORLD

Among the many things for which World War II has become famous are the number of inventions that drastically reshaped the world.

JET AIRCRAFT

In 1930, British engineer Frank Whittle became the first person to file a patent for a jet engine. On August 27, 1937, a few days before it invaded Poland, Germany performed the first jet-propelled flight. The first Allied jet-powered plane took to the skies on May 15, 1941. It would take a while for jet aircraft to be perfected, but once they were, they transformed both civilian and military transportation.

Yet another world-changing innovation arising from the war was the jet airplane, which revolutionized civilian travel as well as military combat.

RADAR

The first workable radar system was developed in 1935 by British physicist Sir Robert Watson-Watt, whose contributions allowed Great Britain to erect a network of radar stations along its south and east coasts. By the 1940s, the Massachusetts Institute of Technology's radiation laboratory, called "Red Lab," had made advances that effectively enabled Allied forces to detect enemy ships and planes. Today, radar is an invaluable tool in detecting both major weather events and hazards in both ship and airplane navigation.

THE COMPUTER

During World War II, the United States began to develop machines to take the place of calculations carried out by hand. The early creators of these machines were predominantly women, most notably Jean Jennings Bartik, who led the way in the development of computer storage and memory; Frances "Betty" Holberton, who created the first software application; and US Navy Lieutenant Grace Hopper, who developed the first computer programming languages. These efforts all led to one of the most important life-altering inventions in history.

PENICILLIN

This lifesaving drug was discovered in 1928 by Scottish scientist Alexander Fleming, but it was not until the war that the United States began to mass-produce it. Regarded by millions as a miracle drug, penicillin was one of the first effective treatments for bacterial infections. It reduced the pain incurred by combatants and greatly increased their chances of survival. The medicine was regarded as so important to the Allies' chances of victory that in preparation for the D-Day invasion, the United States produced 2.3 million doses of the drug. Today, penicillin is as ubiquitous and effective a medication for civilians as it was for those who fought in World War II.

BLOOD PLASMA TRANSFUSION

During World War II, an African American surgeon named Charles Drew succeeded in standardizing the production of blood plasma for medical use. The great invention of blood plasma was that unlike whole blood, plasma can be given to anyone regardless of their blood type, one of the reasons that it remains one of the world's greatest medical discoveries.

The many other inventions to come out of World War II include photocopying machines, ATMs, and ballpoint pens.

One of the greatest and most lifesaving of all the inventions to come out of World War II was blood plasma.

into Milwaukee—the first franchise to move in fifty years. The Braves would change locale again to keep up with the country, leaving a declining Milwaukee in 1966 and settling in Atlanta, the capital of the "New South."

In time, the Dodgers would make their own bold move. In 1957, the team's owner Walter O'Malley announced the unthinkable. The Dodgers, riding the wave of California's surging popularity, were leaving Brooklyn and the hallowed Ebbets Field and moving to Los Angeles. The next year, the Giants also headed to the West Coast, leaving only the Yankees to represent the nation's largest city.

Constant change was quickly becoming the new norm, for both the nation and the game. But through it all, some things about baseball have never changed, and perhaps they never will. The game itself is still batter against pitcher, with ninety feet between the bases. It still resists being rushed. Baseball fans are still mad about statistics. They still love to see new records being set and broken. And they still cherish the history of their game in a way unlike any other sport—a history that is inextricably linked with that of America itself. And one thing is for certain. Whatever changes lie ahead for baseball, its fans will probably always relish returning to the past, and especially to stories like the shining season of 1941, the year when baseball was there for its fans and its country, at the time when they needed their pastime most.

As they have in good times and bad, tens of millions of Americans still rely on the traditions and excitement of baseball to bring them joy and comfort.

FURTHER READING FOR EACH CHAPTER

BASEBALL ON THE BRINK

Hunter, Stephen. "'Hank Greenberg': The Inspiring Tale of a True Tiger." *Washington Post*, May 25, 2000. https://www.washingtonpost.com/archive/lifestyle/2000/05/26/hank-greenberg-the-inspiring-tale-of-a-true-tiger/92bb07e6-68e1-4c05-9cf8-e475c313edb9/.

THE STREAK

Muratore, Elizabeth. "DiMaggio's 56-Game Hit Streak One of the MLB's Most Hallowed Records." MLB, May 15, 2025. https://www.mlb.com/news/joe-dimaggio-56-game-hitting-streak.

THE KID

Cichalski, Dan. "The Day Ted Williams Put His .400 Season on the Line." MLB, September 27, 2022. https://www.mlb.com/news/ted-williams-plays-in-1941-to-hit-406.

SEPIA BALL

Martano, Steven. "A History of the Negro Leagues' East-West All Star Games." SBNation, February 11, 2021. https://www.beyondtheboxscore.com/2021/2/11/22277532/history-of-the-negro-leagues-east-west-all-star-games.

THE WORLD SERIES

Fimrite, Ron. "The Play that Beat the Bums: The 1941 World Series, Between the Brooklyn Dodgers and the New York Yankees, Turned on a Dropped Third Strike." Sports Illustrated Vault, October 20, 1997. https://vault.si.com/vault/1997/10/20/the-play-that-beat-the-bums-the-1941-world-series-between-the-brooklyn-dodgers-and-the-new-york-yankees-turned-on-a-dropped-third-strike.

BASEBALL GOES TO WAR

Jeanes, William. "Baseball in World War II." Sports Illustrated Vault, August 26, 1991. https://vault.si.com/vault/1991/08/26/baseball-in-world-war-ii-fdr-let-baseball-continue-so-we-had-a-pastime-played-by-graybeards-no-beards-and-other-marvels.

JAPAN AND BASEBALL

Elridge, Larry. "A Whole New (Japanese) Ballgame." *The Christian Science Monitor*, July 27, 1989. https://www.csmonitor.com/1989/0727/dbpwa.html.

THE FUTURE BEGINS

Ashford, James. "The Teenager Explained in 60 Seconds: Ideas that Changed the World." *The Week*, updated August 18, 2023. https://www.theweek.co.uk/52-ideas-that-changed-the-world/103249/52-ideas-that-changed-the-world-14-the-teenager.

SOURCES

THE FOLLOWING SOURCES HAVE BEEN PARTICULARLY IMPORTANT IN PRESENTING KEY CONCEPTS IN THIS BOOK

- Two Books, Robert Creamer's *Baseball in '41* and Geoffrey Ward and Ken Burn's *Baseball: An Illustrated History*, provided the most complete insight into the extraordinary 1941 baseball season.

- *Streak* by Michael Seidel and Ted Williams's autobiography *My Turn at Bat* offer the most complete understanding not only of the greatness of two of baseball's most legendary figures but two of the greatest achievements in all of sports history.

- Lawrence D. Hogan's *Shades of Glory* and Larry Lester's *Black Baseball's National Showcase* proved to be invaluable in conveying an understanding of Black baseball in general and the East-West All-Star game in particular.

- There has probably never been a better baseball wordsmith than Roger Angell, and no one has ever better captured the magic of the game than he did in both *The Summer Game* and *Five Seasons: A Baseball Companion*.

- For a full understanding of the role of women in baseball (not softball), there is not a better source than Barbara Gregorich's *Women at Play*.

BIBLIOGRAPHY OF THE MOST SIGNIFICANT SOURCES WE USED IN OUR RESEARCH

Angell, Roger. *Five Seasons: A Baseball Companion.* University of Nebraska Press, 2004.

Angell, Roger. *The Summer Game.* University of Nebraska Press, 2004.

Creamer, Robert W. *Baseball in '41: A Celebration of the "Best Baseball Season Ever."* Viking, 1991.

Golenbock, Peter. *Bums: An Oral History of the Brooklyn Dodgers.* Dover, 1984.

Gregorich, Barbara. *Women at Play: The Story of Women in Baseball.* Hancourt, 1993.

Hogan, Lawrence D. *Shades of Glory: The Negro Leagues and the Story of African-American Baseball.* National Geographic, 2006.

Katz, Harry, Frank Ceresl, and Phil Michel. *Baseball Americana: Treasures from the Library of Congress.* Smithsonian Books, 2009.

Lester, Larry. *Black Baseball's National Showcase: The East-West All-Star Game, 1933–1953.* University of Nebraska Press, 2001.

Ross, Gregory. *America 1941: A Nation at the Crossroads.* Free Press, 1988.

Seidel, Michael. *Streak: Joe DiMaggio and the Summer of '41.* McGraw-Hill, 1988.

Ward, Geoffrey, and Ken Burns. *Baseball: An Illustrated History.* Knopf, 1994.

Williams, Ted, and John Underwood. *My Turn at Bat.* Simon and Schuster, 1969.

ACKNOWLEDGMENTS

The authors wish to thank Jill Heine, Susan Wilson, and Joslyn Quinan for their many contributions to this book. Thanks also to Bob Kendrick, President of the Negro Leagues Baseball Museum, for his guidance in finding the all-too-scanty stats available on Sepia Ball in the 1940s.

A special debt of gratitude is owed to the following members of the Bloomsbury staff: Publishing Director Mary Kate Castellani, Creative Director Donna Mark, Designers Patrick Collins and Diane M. Collins, Senior Production Editor Oona Patrick, Managing Editorial Director Laura Phillips, Production Manager Lisa Hedicker, Editorial Director Sarah Shumway, Director of Educational Marketing Beth Eller, Associate Publicist Emani Glee, Assistant Marketing Manager Briana Williams, School and Library Marketing Associate Tiffany Coelho, copy editor Jeffrey Curry, and proofreader Helen Armalas.

Finally, much appreciation and thanks are due to this book's editor extraordinaire, Megan Abbate. Thank you, Megan, for your insights, your hard work, and your belief in this book. Your contributions shine through on every page.

PHOTOGRAPH CREDITS

ClassicStock/Archive Photos/Getty Images: v; Courtesy of Library of Congress: 1, 5, 6–7, 18, 30, 33, 49, 102, 109, 118, 124, 138, 140 bottom; Bettmann/Getty Images: 2, 14, 20, 22, 24, 25, 26, 36, 37, 38, 40, 41 top, 42, 46, 47, 51, 52, 53 top and bottom, 56, 59 bottom, 74, 84, 91, 92, 93, 96, 97, 106, 108 top, 111 top, 112, 119, 120 left and right, 121 top and bottom, 122, 126, 127, 128, 129, 132, 143, 153, 156, 158, 164, 166, 169, 170, 171, 174; U.S. National Archives: 4, 114, 131, 135; Jeremy Chen/Stringer/Getty Images Sport: 8; Fox Photos/Stringer/Hulton Archive/Getty Images: 9; Corbis Historical/Getty Images: 10, 44; Everett Collection/Bridgeman Images: 13; Pioneer111/iStock/Getty Images: 16-17; tacar/iStock/Getty Images: 16; Transcendental Graphics/Getty Images Sport: 39, 77, 81, 83, 86, 101, 111 bottom, 125, 140 top, 145, 148; Wikimedia Commons: 41 bottom, 62, 89, 147, 150; *Boston Globe*/Getty Images: 45, 160; B Bennett/Getty Images: 48; Darren McCollester/Stringer/Getty Images: 59 top; FPG/Archive Photos/Getty Images: 60; dalton00/iStock/Getty Images: 61; Heritage Images/Hulton Archive/Getty Images: 64, 76; Chicago History Museum/Getty Images: 65; Tamiment Library/New York University/District 65 UAW: 67; Vince Compagnone/Los Angeles Times/Getty Images: 69; Temple University Libraries, Charles L. Blockson Afro-American Collection: 70, 78, 80; Transcendental Graphics/Getty Images: 73; Diamond Images/Getty Images: 94; MLB Photos/Stringer/Getty Images: 98; Sporting News Archive/Getty Images: 99; Sports Studio Photos/Getty Images Sport: 100, 107, 113; Flickr: 105; Underwood Archives/Getty Images: 108, 144; George Rinhart/Corbis Historical/Getty Images: 110, 141; Naval History and Heritage Command: 116; Reg Speller/Stringer/Hulton Archive/Getty Images: 134; The Chevrons and Diamonds Collection: 136; Gary Bedingfield/Baseball in Wartime: 137; Hulton Archive/Stringer/Getty Images: 142; Keystone-France/Getty-Images: 146; US Marine Corps Museum & University of South Carolina Moving Image Research Collection: 151; *New York Times*/Getty Images: 152; Koji Watanabe/Getty Images: 154 top; Atushi Tomura/Getty Images: 154 bottom; Jon Soohoo/Getty Images: 155 top; Albert Dickson/Sporting News/Getty Images: 155 bottom; Archive Holdings Inc./Getty Images: 159; H. Armstrong Roberts/ClassicStock/Getty Images: 161; John Collier/Library of Congress/Getty Images: 162; Three Lions/Hulton Archive/Getty Images: 172; U.S. Department of Defense: 173. Recurring design elements come from bortonia/DigitalVision/Getty Images; KeithBishop/DigitalVision/Getty Images; Photoco/iStock/Getty Images; ChrisGorgio/iStock/Getty Images; Olga_Z/iStock/Getty Images; OLDsquirrel/DigitalVision/Getty Images.

INDEX

Page numbers in *italics* indicate photos.

Africa, 7, 19
African Americans. *See* Black Americans
Aida, Yoichi, 152
Airplanes, 172, *172*
Alexander, Grover Cleveland, *84*
All-American Girls Professional Baseball League (AAGPBL), 123–133, *125–127*
All-Star Games
    in 1941, 50, 51–53, *52*
    Black players at, 54
    great moments of, 54–55
    of Negro Leagues, 72–87, *74–76*, 90
    start of, 50
American dream, 159–160
American League, 4, 50–52, 54–55, 96
Amsterdam Star-News (newspaper), 67, 73, 85, 87
Analytics, 8
Anderson, Dave, 30
Angell, Robert, 111
Antibiotics, 173
Appling, Luke, 29
"Arsenal of democracy," 7, 130
Atlanta Braves, 174
Atomic bombs, 41, 151
Auker, Elden, 32
Automobile, *162*, 162–163

Baby boomers, 168
Bagwell, Jeff, 55
Baker, Del, *53*
Baker, Vernon, 88
Banks, Ernie, *2*
Barber, Red, 100, 104, 105, 106
Bartik, Jean Jennings, 173
Baseball
    in 1941 *vs.* now, 2, 3–4, 8, *8*
    as distraction, 32, 90, 95, 116, 118, 123
    FDR's "Green Light Letter" on, 118
    during Great Depression, 1
    in internment camps, 124, *124*
    in Japan, 139–155, *140*
    media coverage of (*See* Media)

    as "national pastime," iv, 133
    postwar, *160*, 160–161
    and relationship between US and Japan, 139, 151–153
    segregation in, vi, 6, 66, 67, 71, 167
    soldiers playing, *129*, 133–137
    in spring, iv, 1–2, 3
    technological changes in, 165
Baseball (Burr), 116
Baseball clubs/teams. *See also specific clubs/teams*
    in 1941, 3
    in AAGPBL, 125, 129
    Black clubs (*See* Negro Leagues)
    during Great Depression, 1
    local, 5, *6–7*
    spring training by, 1–2, 3, 10
Baseball fans. *See* Fans
Baseball games
    in 1941 *vs.* now, 3–4, 8
    afternoon, 3
    analytics of, 8
    local, 5, *6–7*
    national pride at, *viii*
    night, 100, *102*, 102–103, 161
    pickup games, 5
    radio broadcast of, 4, *4*, 5, 98, 100, 128
    sandlot games, 5, *5*
    television broadcast of, *108*, 133, *164*, 165–166
    tickets to, 4
Baseball in '41 (Creamer), 29–30
Baseball players
    Black Americans as (*See* Black players)
    camaraderie among, 3
    contracts of, 46
    equipment of, 8
    gloves of, 8, *8*
    military draft of, v, 2, 10–11, 15, 79, 115–116, 123
    offseason jobs of, 2, *2*
    salaries of, 2, *2*, 68, 128
    on tour in Japan, 140, 141–147, *152*, 152–153
    traveling by train, 3
    unionization of, 166–167

    as war heroes, 120–121, *120–121*
    in war years, 119, 122
    women as, vi, 123–133, *125–127*
Baseball season of 1941
    DiMaggio's hitting streak in, 23–24, 27–40, *39*
    as distraction, v, 32, 90, 95
    of Negro Leagues, 66, 72–87
    president's public address during game in, 15–19
    spring training in, 1–2, 3, 10
    story of, v–vi
    Williams' batting average record in, 43, 56–60
    World Series, *94*, 95, 105–113, *108–113*
Basketball, 166
Battan, Eddie, 106
Batting averages, 23
    of DiMaggio (Joe), 21–22, 25, 40
    now, 61
    of Williams (Ted), 46, 48–50, 53, 56–60
    Williams' (Ted) record, 43, 56–60
Bell, Cool Papa, 93, *93*
"Belles of the Ball Game," 126
Berra, Yogi, 121, *121*, 144
Birmingham Black Barons, 85
Black Americans
    as fans, vi, 73–76, 79, 85, 87
    fighting in World War II, 88, *89*, 167
    in Great Depression, 65
    military draft of, 12–13
    in postwar America, 159, 160, 167, 171
Black newspapers, 66–67, 72
Black players, 63–93
    at All-Star games, 54
    challenges of, 68–69
    in GI World Series, 135
    in Hall of Fame, 82, 93
    league of, vi, 6, 66 (*See also* Negro Leagues)
    in major leagues, 71–72, 79, 81, 90–93, 167–170
    in Mexican League, 68, 80–81, *81*
Blackwell, Ewell "the Whip," 135

Blood plasma transfusion, 173, *173*
Blue, Vida, 55
Bombing raids (World War II), 6–7, *9*, 18, *24*
Bonham, Ernie "Tiny," 112–113
Bostic, Joe, 67
Boston Braves, 15, 120, 171
Boston Red Sox, 27, 37–38, 44
Boudreau, Lou, 41, 50
Brett, George, 61
Broadcasting
   radio, 4, *4*, 5, 98, 100, 128
   television, *108*, 133, *164*, 165–166
"Bronx Bombers." *See* New York Yankees
Brooklyn Dodgers, 96–105
   ballpark of, 104–105
   Black players in, 71, 81, 90, 167
   entertaining style of, 104
   fans of, 104–107, *106*, *107*, *110*
   ineptitude of, 97–98
   move of, *171*, 174
   nickname of, 97
   slogan of, 98
   transformation of, 98–101
   during war years, 119
   in World Series of 1941, 95, 105–113
Brown, Tommy, 119
Brown, Willard, 135, 136, 137
"Buffalo Soldiers," 88, *89*
Burley, Dan, 67, 72
Burr, Harold, 116

Caligiuri, Fred, 59
Camilli, Dolph, *100*, 104
Campanella, Roy, 54, *78*, 78–79, 86, 90–91, *91*
Carew, Rod, 61
Cars, *162*, 162–163
Carter, Art, 87
Casey, Hugh, 108, 109–110
Chandler, Spud, *108*
Chapman, Ben, 119
Cheerios, 16
Chester, Hilda, 106–107
Chicago Cubs, 123, 155
Chicago Defender (newspaper), 67, 72, 73, 76, 85
Chicago White Sox, 8, 28, 29
China, 7, *10*, 117

Churchill, Winston, *24*
Cincinnati Reds, 119, *119*, 171
Cleveland Indians, 28, 38–40, 92, 120
Cochrane, Mickey, 141
Combs, Earle, 28
Computers, 172–173
Conn, Billy, 31
Courtney, Alan, 30
Creamer, Robert, 29–30, 41, 98
Cronin, Joe, 37, 54, 56, 57, 60
Cunningham, Bill, 45

"Daffiness Boys." *See* Brooklyn Dodgers
Dahlgren, Babe, 34
Daniel, Dan, 106–107
Darvish, Yu, 155
Davis, "Pepper" Paire, 125
Davis, Ralph, 103
Day, Leon, 135, 136, 137
Deferment, 15
Detroit Tigers
   in 1941, 27, 31, 32, 96
   in 1944, 123
   player drafted from, 10–11, 15
Diaz, Joe, 5
Dickey, Bill, 21, 96, 111
DiMaggio, Dom, 38, 51, 144
DiMaggio, Joe, *20*, *22*, *37*, *39*, *41*, *51*
   at All-Star Game, 50, 51–52
   in Baseball Hall of Fame, *41*
   bat of, *30*
   batting average of, 21–22, 25, 40
   batting style of, 23, *25*
   early accomplishments of, 21–22
   family of, 21
   Henrich (Tommy) on, 40–41
   hitting streak of, 23–24, 27–40, *39*
   in Japan, 144
   nicknames of, 23, 30
   on Paige (Satchel), 79
   personality of, 22, 31
   pressure felt by, 30–31
   in World Series of 1941, 96, *96*, *108*, 111, *112*, 113
Doby, Larry, 54, *91*
Doerr, Bobby, 50
Draft. *See* Military draft
Drew, Charles, 173
Durocher, Leo, 71, *99*, 99, 107, 119

East-West All-Star Game, 72–87, *74–76*, 90
Ebbets Field, 104–105
England. *See* Great Britain

Fans
   in 1941, 4
   of AAGPBL, *127*, 128, 129, 133
   Black Americans as, vi, 73–76, 79, 85, 87
   of Brooklyn Dodgers, 104–107, *106*, *107*, *110*
   of DiMaggio (Joe), 25, 28, 30, 31, 36–39
   FDR as, 116, *118*
   in Japan, 141, 143, 145, 147
   of local teams, 5, *6–7*
   of Negro Leagues, 73–76, 79, 85, 87
   in spring, iv
   on Williams (Ted), 44–45
   women as, *4*, 5
Faut, Jean, 128
Feller, Bob, *20*, 50, 120, *120*
Fighting Ninety-Second Division, 88, *89*
Fincher, Jack, 126
"Fireside chats," 7
Fish, Hamilton, 19
Fitzsimmons, "Fat Freddie," 108
Fleming, Alexander, 173
Football, 166
Foster, Rube, 64, *65*
Fowler, Dick, 58
Fox, John R., 88
Fox, Nelson, 119
Fox, Pete, 27
Foxx, Jimmie, 44, 54, 147
Freedman, Lew, 29

Gacioch, Rose, 126
Galbreath, Elizabeth, 73
Gedeon, Elmer, 121
Gehrig, Lou, 34, 54, 76, 141, *142*, 147
Geringher, Charlie, 147
Germany
   bombing raids by, 6–7, *9*, 18, *24*
   Europe occupied by, iv–v, 6, 18–19
   and Japan, 7, 117
   ships sunk by, 19, 24, *105*
   Soviet Union attacked by, 24, 31–32
   surrender of, 134
GI Bill, 158, *158*, 168

GI World Series, 134–137, *136, 137*
Gibson, Josh, 78, *80,* 80–81, *81,* 93
Gloves, 8, *8*
Golenbock, Peter, 107
Gomez, Lefty, 21, 96
"Goodwill tours," 140, 141–147, *152,* 152–153
Gordon, Joe, 21, *22,* 51, 96, *96,* 111
Gottlieb, Eddie, 77
Gould, Stephen Jay, 60
Gray, Pete, *122*
Great Britain
    American soldiers playing baseball in, 133, *134*
    US sending military supplies to, 7, 19, 27
    in World War II, v, 6–7, *9,* 18, *24*
Great Depression, 1, 65
"Green Light Letter" (Roosevelt), 118
Greenberg, Hank, 10–11, *14,* 15, 115–116
Greenberg, Joe, 11, 15
Greenlee, Gus, 72
Griffey, Ken, 55
Grimm, Charlie, 128
"Ground rule double," 58, 59
Grove, Lefty, 37, 141
Gutteridge, Don, 3

Hall of Fame, *41, 59,* 65, 82, 93, *93*
Harnett, Gabby, 71
Harris, Ed, 67
Henrich, Tommy
    on DiMaggio's hitting streak, 32–33, 40–41
    in World Series of 1941, 108, 109–110, *111,* 113
    in Yankees 1941 lineup, 21, *22,* 96, *96*
Herman, Babe, 98, 119
Herman, Billy, *100*
Higbe, Kirby, 104
Hitler, Adolf, 6, 67
Hitting streak of DiMaggio, 23–24, 27–40, *39*
Holberton, Frances "Betty," 173
Home runs, 34, *52,* 54–55
Homer, Ben, 30
Homestead Grays, 77, 81
Hopper, Grace, 173
Hornsby, Rogers, 44
Hubbell, Carl, 19, 50, 54

Hunter, Stephen, 11

Internment camps, 124, *124*
Irvin, Monte, *70*
    in East-West All-Star Game (1941), 87, 90
    in Hall of Fame, 93
    on Leonard (Buck), 77
    in major leagues, 91, *92*
    in Mexican League, 80
    scout report on, 71–72
Ishimaru, Shinichi, 149, *150*
Italy, iv–v, 7, 32, 88, 117

Jackson, Reggie, 55
Japan
    atomic bombings of, 151
    attack on Pearl Harbor by, *114,* 115, 117, 148
    baseball in, 139–155, *140*
    baseball players serving in military of, 149–151
    "goodwill tours" in, 140, 141–147, *152,* 152–153
    isolation of, 139, 141
    militarism in, 144, 148
    in World War II, v, 7–9, *10,* 117
Japanese Americans
    internment of, 124, *124*
    in major leagues, 154–155
Jet aircraft, 172, *172*
Johnson, Bob, 58
Johnson, Judy, 103
Johnson, Susan E., 128
"Joltin' Joe DiMaggio" (song), 30
Jukeboxes, *163*

Kamenshek, Dorothy, *125,* 126–127
Kansas City Monarchs, 82, 102–103
Kansas City Royals, 34
Keeler, "Wee Willie," 31, 36–38
Keller, Charlie, 21, *22,* 96, *96,* 111
Keltner, Ken, 38–40, 51
Kendrick, Bob, 82, 103
Kenosha Comets, 125
"The Kid." *See* Williams, Ted
Kimbro, "Jimbo," 85
Knox, Frank, *13*
Kuenster, Robert, 61
Kurys, Sophie, *126,* 127
Kyojin-gun, 149

Labor unions, 166–167
Lacy, Sam, 67, 72
LaGuardia, Fiorello, 19
Landis, Kenesaw Mountain, 116, 118
Landon, Alf, 19
Larkin, Barry, 55
Lavagetto, Cookie, 106
Lee, Thornton, 8
LeMahieu, DJ, 34
Leonard, Buck, 76–78, *77,* 85, 87, 90, 93
Leonard, Dutch, 36
Local baseball teams, 5, *6–7*
Lodigiani, Dario, 28
Lopez, Al, 61
Los Angeles Dodgers, 155, *171,* 174
Lottery (military draft), 9–10, 12, *13*
Louis, Joe, 31

MacArthur, Douglas, 151–152
Mack, Connie, 58
MacPhail, Larry, 98–100
Manley, Effa, 65, *73*
Martin, Pepper, 119
Martinez, Pedro, 55
Matsui, Hideki, *154,* 155
Mays, Willie, 91, *92*
McCarthy, Joe, 33, *41*
McGwire, Mark, 55
McNearney, Allison, 163
Media. *See also* Newspapers; Radio; Television
    in 1941, 2, 4–5, 29, *108, 109*
    on women's baseball, 128–129
Mexican League, 68, 80–81, *81*
Military draft, iv
    in 1940, 9–15
    in 1941, 35, 36
    of baseball players, v, 2, 10–11, 15, 79, 115–116, 123
    of Black Americans, 12–13, 79
    deferment from, 15
    exemptions from, 13
    lottery used in, 9–10, 12, *13*
    registering for, 11, 36
    requirements for, 12
    unfit for, 122
Milwaukee Braves, 174
Minneapolis Millers, 44
Mize, Johnny, 50
M&Ms, 16
Moore, Terry, 3

Morrow, Lance, 159–160
Mulcahy, Hugh "Losing Pitcher," v, 10
Murakami, Masanori, 154, *154*
Musial, Stan, 55

Nahem, Sam, 135
National Baseball Hall of Fame, *41, 59,* 65, 82, 93
National League, 4, 51–52, 54–55, 101
National pride, *viii, 26*
Negro American League, 65, 66, 77
Negro Leagues
    1941 season of, 66, 72–87
    All-Star Game of, 72–87, *74–75*
    challenges of, 68–69
    fans of, 73–76, 79, 85, 87
    history of, 64–65
    night baseball introduced by, *102,* 102–103
    players leaving for Mexican League, 80–81, 86
Negro National League (NNL), 64–65, 66
New York Giants, 15, 71–72, 91, *92,* 144
New York Times, 95, *105,* 136, *163*
New York Yankees
    1941 lineup of, 21, *22,* 96, *96*
    on broadcasting, 5
    dominance of, 95–96
    hitting streak record of, 28, *39*
    home run record of, 34
    Matsui (Hideki) in, 155
    nickname of, 21
    during war years, 119
    in World Series of 1941, 95, 105–113
Newark Eagles, 65
Newcombe, Don, 54, 90, *91*
Newhouser, Hal, 27, 32
Newsom, Bobo, 31
Newsome, Dick, 37
Newspapers
    on AAGPBL, 129
    on baseball in Japan, 147
    on baseball in war years, 116
    Black newspapers, 66–67, 72
    on DiMaggio's hitting streak, 29, *33, 38, 40*
    on GI World Series, 136–137
    on Williams (Ted), 45, *49,* 53, 56–57, 59, 60

Nomo, Hideo, 154–155, *155*
Nuremberg, GI World Series in, 135–137, *136*
Nuxhall, Joe, 119, *119*

O'Doul, Lefty, 143, 144, *144,* 149, 152–153, *153*
Ohtani, Shohei, 154, *154*
Omachi, George, 124
O'Malley, Walter, 174
O'Neil, Buck, 76, 79
O'Neil, Harry, 121
Operation Magic Carpet, 158
Orlando, Johnny, 57
Ott, Mel, 43, 50
Overseas Invasion Service Expedition (OISE) All-Stars, 135–137, *137*
Owen, Mickey, 105–108, 109, 110–111, *111*

Paige, Satchel, 68, 79–82, *83, 84,* 87, 92, 93
Palmero, Rafael, 34
Pasquel, Jorge, 80, 81
Passeau, Claude, 51, 52
Pearl Harbor attack (1941), *114,* 115, 117, 148
Peckinpaugh, Roger, 28
Penicillin, 173
Philadelphia Athletics, 35, 56–60, 119
Philadelphia Bobbies, 140, *141*
Philadelphia Phillies, v, 10, 119
Philadelphia Royal Giants, 140
Pickup baseball, 5
Pierce, Jack, 106
Pipp, Wally, 126
Pitchers, 8
Pittsburgh Courier (newspaper), 67, 76, 86
Pittsburgh Pirates, 167
Poland, 6, 24
Povich, Shirley, 67, 71
Prices, in 1941 vs now, *16–17*

"Queens of Swat," 126

Racine Belles, 125, *126,* 127
Racism, vi, 6
Radar, 172
Radcliffe, Ted "Double Duty," 68, 69

Radio
    baseball games on, 4, *4,* 5, 98, 100, 128
    on DiMaggio's hitting streak, 30
    FDR addressing people on, 7, 15–19, 27
Red Circlers, 135–137
Reese, Pee Wee, *97,* 100, 108
Reiser, Pete, *101,* 104, 107, 109
Rickard, Tex, 105
Rickey, Branch, 167, 169
Rigney, Johnny, 28
Rizzuto, Phil, 96, *98,* 108
Robinson, Jackie, 54, 71, 81, *91, 169,* 169–170, *170*
Rockford Peaches, 125, *125,* 126
Rodriguez, Alex, 34
Rodriguez, Ivan, 34
Rolfe, Red, 32, 33
Roosevelt, Franklin D. (FDR), *18*
    as baseball fan, 116, *118*
    "fireside chats" by, 7
    GI Bill of Rights signed by, 158, *158*
    "Green Light Letter" of, 118
    public address by, 15–19, 27
Rosenthal, Larry, 39
Round-trippers, 34, 58, 96
Ruffing, Red, 21, 50, 96
Russia. *See* Soviet Union
Russo, Marius, 32, 108
Ruth, Babe, 22, 48, *48,* 54, 143–147, *145, 146,* 148

Salaries, 2, *2,* 68, 128
Sams, Doris, 126
San Diego Padres, 44, 155
San Francisco Giants, 154, 174
San Francisco Seals, 143, 144, 152–153
Sanchez, Gary, 34
Sandlot games, 5, *5*
Sawamura, Eiji, 147, *147,* 148, 150–151
Scheib, Carl, 119
Schroeder, Dottie, 128
Seattle Mariners, 155
Second World War. *See* World War II
Segregation
    in baseball, vi, 6, 66, 67, 71, 167
    protests against, *67,* 71
    in society, 63, 167
Seidel, Michael, 23
Selective Training and Service Act (1940), 12

Sepia Ball, 66, *76*
Setup pitchers, 8
Seventy-First Division, 134–137
Shoriki, Matsutaro, 148
Simmons, Al, 54, 141
Sisler, George, 31, 32, 35–36
Smith, Al, 38
Smith, Eddie, 25
Smith, Hilton, 82–85, *86,* 91–92
Smith, Red, 113
Smith, Wendell, 67
Sosa, Sammy, 55
South Bend Blue Sox, 125
Soviet Union, 24, 31–32
Spahn, Warren, 120, *120*
Spence, Stan, 37
"Splendid Splinter." *See* Williams, Ted
Sporting News, 106, 107, 148, 161
Spring, baseball in, iv, 1–2, *3*
Spring training, 1–2, 3, 10
St. Louis Browns, 32–33, 119–123, *122*
St. Louis Cardinals, 101, 119, 123
Starting pitchers, 8
Stengel, Casey, 23
Stewart, Riley, 68
Stimson, Henry, 12
Stoneham, Horace, 71–72
Strong, Ted, 85
Sturm, Johnny, 32, 34, 109
Suburbs, 158–159, *159*
Suzuki, Ichiro, 55, 155, *155*

Taylor, Candy Jim, 84
Technology
   in 1941 *vs.* now, 2
   postwar changes in, 161–166, 171
"Teddy Ballgame." *See* Williams, Ted
Teenagers, *162,* 162–163, *163*
Telephone, 171
Television, *108,* 133, *164,* 165–166, 171
Texas Rangers, 34, 155
Thompson, Hank, *92*
Tokyo Giants, 148, 149
"Toothpick Ted." *See* Williams, Ted
Trains, 3
Truman, Harry S., 171

Umpire, 8, *62*
Uniforms, *8,* 149
United Kingdom. *See* Great Britain

"Unlimited national emergency," 19, 27

Vaccaro, Mike, 15
Van Robays, Maurice, 135
Vander Meer, Johnny, 100
Vaughan, Arky, 51, *100*
Vaughan, Porter, 58
Veeck, Bill, 92

Wagner, Audrey, 128
Wakefield, Dick, 123
Walker, Harry "the Hat," 135, 136
Walker, Larry, 55
Warner, Paul, 119
Washington Afro-American (newspaper), 85, 86, 87
Washington Senators, 35–36, 56
Watson-Watt, Sir Robert, 172
Weintraub, Robert, 137
Wells, Willie, *80*
When Women Played Hardball (Johnson), 128
Whittle, Frank, 172
Wilkinson, JL, 102–103
Williams, Ted, *42, 44, 47, 48, 51, 53*
   at All-Star Game, 50, 51–53, *52*
   in Baseball Hall of Fame, *59*
   batting average of, 46, 48–50, 53, 56–60
   batting average record of, 43, 56–60
   batting style of, 46–47, *53*
   concentration of, 46, 47
   on DiMaggio (Joe), 23
   early years of, 43–44
   eyesight of, *56*
   fans on, 44–45
   on inclusion of Black players in Hall of Fame, 93
   as military hero, *60,* 121, *121*
   nicknames of, 44, 59
   personality of, 44–45
   pressure felt by, 53–56, 57–58
   rookie card of, *45*
   tribute to, *59*
Williams Shift, 46
"Willowy Walloper." *See* Williams, Ted
Wilson, Horace, 139
Women
   as baseball fans, *4,* 5
   as baseball players, vi, 123–133, *125–127*
   as computer programmers, 173

   in Hall of Fame, 65
   wartime jobs of, 130–131, *131*
World Series, 4
   of 1941, *94,* 95, 105–113, *108–113*
   GI, 134–137, *136, 137*
World War II
   atomic bombs in, 41, 151
   Black Americans fighting in, 88, *89,* 167
   bombing raids in, 6–7, *9,* 18, *24*
   events in, 6–9
   inventions of, 172–173
   Japanese American internment in, 124, *124*
   Pearl Harbor attack, *114,* 115, 117, 148
   situation in 1941, iv–v, 6, 18–19, 24, 90, *105*
   soldiers playing baseball during, *129,* 133–137
   start of, 6
   US after, 157–174
Wrigley, Phillip, 123
Wyatt, Whitlow, 104, 106, *112*
Wyrostek, Johnny, 135

Yakyu (baseball in Japan), 139–155
"Yankee Clipper." *See* DiMaggio, Joe
York, Rudy, 31
Yoshihara, Masaki, 149–150